CATECHISM

FOR THE
PAROCHIAL SCHOOLS
OF THE
UNITED STATES

BY

REV. W. FAERBER

TAN Books
Charlotte, North Carolina

Imprimatur: ✠ Joseph E. Ritter, S.T.D.
Archbishop of St. Louis

February 28, 1958

Library of Congress Catalog Card Number: 78-68498

ISBN: 978-0-89555-086-6

TAN Books
Charlotte, North Carolina
www.TANBooks.com
2015

CONTENTS

PART III

WE MUST USE THE MEANS OF GRACE

PART IV

LITURGY

INTRODUCTION

1. Who made us?

God made us.

2. Why did God make us?

God made us that we might serve Him and thereby gain heaven.

"What does it profit a man, if he gain the whole world, but suffer the loss of his own soul? Or what will a man give in exchange for his soul?" (Matt. 16:26.)

3. What does God want of us?

God wants of us:

1. that we believe all that He has revealed;
2. that we keep the commandments;
3. that we receive the sacraments, and pray.

Hence the catechism is divided into three parts.

Application. Christ said: "But one thing is necessary." This one necessary thing is to serve God and save our soul. We cannot serve God unless we first know and love Him. We serve God by practicing the true religion. We learn our holy religion in the catechism. "I count all things but loss for the excellent knowledge of Jesus Christ, my Lord" (Phil. 3:8).

PART I

WE MUST BELIEVE ALL THAT GOD HAS REVEALED

THE APOSTLES' CREED

4. Where do we find the chief truths which God has revealed?

We find the chief truths which God has revealed in the Apostles' Creed.

Creed=prayer in which we profess our faith.　Act of faith.

5. Recite the Apostles' Creed.

1. I believe in God, the Father Almighty, Creator of heaven and earth;

2. and in Jesus Christ His only Son, our Lord;

3. who was conceived by the Holy Ghost, born of the Virgin Mary;

4. suffered under Pontius Pilate, was crucified; died and was buried;

5. He descended into hell; the third day He arose again from the dead;

6. He ascended into heaven; sitteth at the right hand of God, the Father Almighty;

7. from thence He shall come to judge the living and the dead.

8. I believe in the Holy Ghost;

9. the Holy Catholic Church, the communion of saints;

10. the forgiveness of sins;

11. the resurrection of the body;

12. and life everlasting.　Amen.

FAITH

FIRST ARTICLE OF THE CREED

I believe in God, the Father Almighty, Creator of heaven and earth

6. What is meant by the word "believe"?

"Believe" means to hold as true all that God has revealed.

7. What has God revealed?

God has revealed what we must know and do to gain heaven.

Revealed=made known.

8. Who teaches us what God has revealed?

The Catholic Church teaches us what God has revealed.

"Go ye into the whole world and preach the gospel to every creature" (Mark 16:15).

9. Is faith necessary to salvation?

Faith is necessary to salvation.

"He that believeth not shall be condemned" (Mark 16:16).

Application. We should thank God for the gift of faith. God gave us the grace to believe. He infused faith into our soul at baptism. We ought to learn well what we must believe.

GOD

10. What is God?

God is the highest and most perfect Spirit from whom all good things come.

A spirit has understanding and free will, but has no body.

11. Why do we say that God is eternal?

We say that God is eternal because He is always; He is without beginning and without end.

"Before the mountains were made, or the earth and the world were formed, from eternity and to eternity Thou art God" (Ps. 89:2).

12. Where is God?

God is everywhere: He is in heaven, on earth, and in all places.

"Whither shall I go from Thy Spirit? Or whither shall I flee from Thy face? If I ascend into heaven, Thou art there; if I descend into hell, Thou art there" (Ps. 138:7, 8).

13. What does God know?

God knows all things: He knows what has been, what is now, and what will be or may be.

"For all things were known to the Lord before they were created; so also after they were perfected He beholdeth all things" (Ecclus. 23:29).

14. Why do we say that God is all-wise?

We say that God is all-wise because He arranges all things in the best way.

"Thou has made all things in wisdom" (Ps. 103:24).

15. What can God do?

God can do everything He wills.

"No word shall be impossible with God" (Luke 1:37).

16. Why do we say that God is holy?

We say that God is holy because He loves and wills only what is good and hates what is evil.

17. Why do we say that God is just?

We say that God is just because He gives to every one what he deserves: He rewards the good and punishes the wicked.

"Who without respect of persons judgeth according to everyone's work" (I Peter 1:17).

18. Why do we say that God is kind?

We say that God is kind because He gives us many blessings since He loves us.

"Every best gift, and every perfect gift, is from above, coming down from the Father of lights" (Jas. 1:17).

19. Why do we say that God is merciful?

We say that God is merciful because He willingly pardons us if we are truly sorry for our sins.

"As I live, saith the Lord, I desire not the death of the sinner, but that the wicked turn from his way and live" (Ezech. 33:11).

Examples: David, Magdalen, the penitent thief.

Parables: Good shepherd (Luke 15:1); prodigal son (Luke 15:11); barren fig tree (Luke 13:6).

20. Why do we say that God is faithful?

We say that God is faithful because He keeps His promises and carries out His threats.

"Heaven and earth shall pass, but My words shall not pass" (Matt. 24:35).

God is incomprehensible, indescribable, unchanging, truthful, long-suffering. His perfections are without number.

Application. We should take a delight in thinking about God. Consideration of His perfections can make saints of us. We should be glad that we are God's adopted children; we should love Him, respect Him, and have confidence in Him.

THE BLESSED TRINITY

21. Is there more than one God?

There is but one God.

"I am the Lord thy God. Thou shalt not have strange gods before Me" (Exod. 20:2).

22. How many persons are there in God?

There are three persons in God: the Father, the Son, and the Holy Ghost.

"Going therefore, teach ye all nations, baptizing them in the name of the Father, and of the Son, and of the Holy Ghost" (Matt. 28:19).

A person is a being who is able to think.

23. Is each of the three Persons true God?

Each of the three Persons is true God.

24. Are these three Persons only one God?

These three Persons are only one God.

"I and the Father are one" (John 10:30).

25. What do we call one God in three Persons?

We call one God in three Persons, the Blessed Trinity.

"There are three that bear witness in heaven: the Father, the Word, and the Holy Ghost: and these three are one" (I John 5:7).

Trinity=three in one.

26. What benefits have the three divine Persons bestowed upon us?

God the Father created us;

God the Son redeemed us;

God the Holy Ghost sanctifies us.

Application. Whenever we make the sign of the cross we profess our faith in the Blessed Trinity. Therefore we should always make it devoutly. We must lead a good life so that we will have the happiness to see and enjoy the Blessed Trinity in eternity.

THE WORLD

27. Who created heaven and earth?

God created heaven and earth.

Create=make out of nothing. Creator. Creature.

28. How do we know that God is the Creator of all things?

We know that God is the Creator of all things from common sense, conscience, and divine revelation.

"The fool hath said in his heart: There is no God" (Ps. 13:1).

29. Why did God make all things?

God made all things for His own glory and for our benefit.

30. What do we mean when we say that God preserves the world?

When we say that God preserves the world, we mean that He keeps it in existence by His all-powerful will.

31. What do we mean when we say that God governs the world?

When we say that God governs the world, we mean that He directs all things according to His wisdom.

Divine Providence.

32. Can anything happen without the will or permission of God?

Nothing can happen without the will or permission of God.

"Are not two sparrows sold for a farthing? And not one of them shall fall on the ground without your Father. But the very hairs of your head are all numbered" (Matt. 10:29, 30).

33. Why does God permit sin?

God permits sin because He has given man free will.

Application. Divine Providence cares for all things, especially man. "Casting all your care upon Him, for He has care of you" (I Pet. 5:7). God knows how to turn evil into good. Sufferings are profitable for both the good and the wicked. "To them that love God, all things work together unto good" (Rom. 8:28).

34. Which are the invisible creatures?

The invisible creatures are the angels.

The nine choirs: angels, archangels, principalities; powers, virtues, dominations; thrones, cherubim, and seraphim.

35. What gifts did God give to the angels?

God gave to the angels: much knowledge, great power, and especially sanctifying grace.

Examples: the three young men in the fiery furnace; Peter delivered from prison.

36. Did all the angels remain good?

Not all the angels remained good; many became proud and refused to serve God.

37. How did God punish the angels who committed sin?

God punished the angels who committed sin by casting them into hell forever.

Devil, Satan, Lucifer; demons, evil spirits.

38. What do the good angels do?

The good angels praise and serve God; and love and help us.

39. Who are the angels that especially protect us?

The angels that especially protect us are our guardian angels.

"Their angels in heaven always see the face of My Father" (Matt. 18:10).

40. What should we do to honor our guardian angel?

To honor our guardian angel we should pray to him daily and heed his promptings.

See prayer on page 97.

41. What does the devil do against us?

The devil tempts us to sin in order to bring us into hell.

"Your adversary the devil, as a roaring lion, goeth about, seeking whom he may devour" (I Pet. 5:8).

42. What should we do to keep the devil from harming us?

To keep the devil from harming us we should watch and pray.

"Watch ye, and pray that you enter not into temptation" (Mark 14:38).

Obsession. Exorcism.

Application. We ought to love our guardian angel, praying to him night and morning, and particularly when tempted. In dangers of soul and body we need not fear; our guardian angel is always near us.

MAN

43. What is man?

Man is a creature composed of body and soul.

44. What is the soul?

The soul is an immortal spirit having understanding and free will.

"Let us make man to our image and likeness" (Gen. 1:26).

"Thou has made him a little less than the angels" (Ps. 8:6).

45. Who were our first parents?

Our first parents were Adam and Eve.

46. How did God make Adam?

God made the body of Adam out of the earth, and breathed an immortal soul into it.

"And the Lord God formed man of the slime of the earth; and breathed into his face the breath of life, and man became a living soul" (Gen. 2:7).

47. What special gift did God give our first parents?

God gave our first parents the special gift of sanctifying grace.

48. What did sanctifying grace do for our first parents?

Sanctifying grace made our first parents adopted children of God and heirs of heaven.

Natural gifts; keen intellect and freedom from evil passions, suffering, and death.

Supernatural gifts: adopted children of God and heirs of heaven.

49. Did our first parents receive sanctifying grace for themselves only?

Our first parents received sanctifying grace not only for themselves; all mankind was to inherit it from them.

50. Why has no one inherited sanctifying grace from Adam and Eve?

No one has inherited sanctifying grace from Adam and Eve because they lost it by committing sin.

"Of every tree of paradise thou shalt eat; but of the tree of the knowledge of good and evil thou shalt not eat" (Gen. 2:16, 17).

51. What punishment did they receive for this sin?

In punishment for this sin they were no longer children of God and heirs of heaven; they were driven from paradise and were subject to suffering and death.

"Cursed is the earth in thy work. Thorns and thistles shall it bring forth to thee. In the sweat of thy face thou shalt eat bread till thou return to the earth, out of which thou wast taken; for dust thou art, and into dust thou shalt return" (Gen. 3:17-19).

52. What then do all men inherit from Adam?

From Adam all men inherit original sin.

"By one man sin entered into this world, and by sin death; and so death passed upon all men, in whom all have sinned" (Rom. 5:12).

53. What are the consequences of original sin?

The consequences of original sin are especially these:

1. before they are baptized, men are not children of God;
2. without baptism, they have no right to heaven;
3. their understanding is darkened, especially in matters of religion;
4. they are inclined to evil;
5. they are subject to many sufferings;
6. they must all die.

54. Who alone was preserved from original sin?

The Blessed Virgin Mary alone was preserved from original sin.

Immaculate Conception.

55. What would have happened if God had not shown mercy to man?

If God had not shown mercy, no man would have entered heaven.

"There shall not enter into it anything defiled" (Apoc. 21:27).

56. How did God show mercy to man?

God showed mercy to man by promising him a Redeemer.

"I will put enmities between thee and the woman, and thy seed and her seed; she shall crush thy head, and thou shalt lie in wait for her heel" (Gen. 3:15).

Redeemer=Savior=one who saves.

Application. Let us hate sin. It was sin that drove our first parents from paradise and brought every evil into the world. We should remember that our soul is an image of God, and keep it free from sin.

JESUS CHRIST

SECOND AND THIRD ARTICLES OF THE CREED

And in Jesus Christ, His only Son, our Lord; who was conceived by the Holy Ghost, born of the Virgin Mary

57. When did the promised Redeemer come?

The promised Redeemer came about two thousand years ago.

58. Who is the promised Redeemer?

Jesus Christ is the promised Redeemer.

Jesus=Savior.   Christ=anointed; Messiah.

"Thou shalt call His name Jesus: for He shall save His people from their sins" (Matt. 1:21).

"There is no other name under heaven given to men whereby we must be saved" (Acts 4:12).

59. Who is Jesus Christ?

Jesus Christ is the Son of God, who was made man for us.

God-man.   One person, divine.   Two natures, divine and human.

Nature=what makes a being to be what it is and act as it does.

60. Who is the mother of Jesus Christ?

The mother of Jesus Christ is the Blessed Virgin Mary.

"The Holy Ghost shall come upon thee, and the power of the Most High shall overshadow thee. And therefore also the Holy which shall be born of thee shall be called the Son of God" (Luke 1:35).

Incarnation.   Feast of the Annunciation, March 25.

61. Who was St. Joseph?

St. Joseph was the spouse of Mary, and the foster-father of Jesus.

Patron of prayer, purity, happy death, laborers, the Church.

62. Why did the Son of God become man?

The Son of God became man to be our teacher, our model, and our Redeemer.

"I am the way, and the truth, and the life" (John 14:6).

63. Where was Jesus born?

Jesus was born in a stable at Bethlehem.

Feast of the Nativity, Christmas, December 25.

Feast of the Circumcision, January 1.

Feast of the Epiphany, January 6.

Feast of the Holy Family, first Sunday after Epiphany.

See the joyful mysteries of the rosary, page 91.

64. What did Jesus do until He was thirty years old?

Until He was thirty years old, Jesus lived at Nazareth and was subject to Mary and Joseph.

"He went down with them and came to Nazareth, and was subject to them" (Luke 2:51).

First thirty years, hidden life.

65. What did Jesus do when He was thirty years old?

When He was thirty years old, Jesus began to teach in public.

Public life, three years.

66. What did Jesus teach about Himself?

Jesus taught that He is the promised Redeemer and the Son of God.

"I and the Father are one" (John 10:30). "Again the high priest asked Him, and said to Him: Art Thou the Christ, the Son of the blessed God? And Jesus said to him: I am" (Mark 14:61, 62).

67. How did Jesus prove that He is the Son of God?

Jesus proved that He is the Son of God:
1. by His very holy life;
2. by His prophecies;
3. by His miracles.

"Which of you shall convince Me of sin?" (John 8:46.)

Prophecies: treason of Judas, Petcr's denial, His own death and resurrection.

Miracle=a temporary suspension of a law of nature; only God can suspend a law of nature.

Application. We cannot be saved except through Jesus Christ. We call Him "our Lord" because He created and redeemed us. We should read the story of His life as recorded in the four Gospels. We should be loyal to Christ all the days of our life, for He is the Son of God and our King.

PASSION AND DEATH OF CHRIST

FOURTH ARTICLE OF THE CREED

Suffered under Pontius Pilate, was crucified, died, and was buried.

68. Which were the chief sufferings of Jesus?

The chief sufferings of Jesus were:
1. the bloody sweat in the garden;
2. the scourging at the pillar;
3. the crowning with thorns;
4. the carrying of the cross;
5. the crucifixion.

Holy Week. Good Friday. The fourteen stations of the cross. The five wounds. The seven last words. The sorrowful mysteries of the rosary.

69. Why did Jesus die on the cross?

Jesus died on the cross

1. to redeem us from sin and hell;
2. to earn for us grace and salvation.

"He was offered because it was His own will" (Is. 53:7).

"Behold the Lamb of God, behold Him who taketh away the sin of the world!" (John 1:29).

70. For whom did Jesus die?

Jesus died for all men.

"Christ died for all" (II Cor. 5:15).

71. What was done with the body of Jesus after death?

After death, the body of Jesus was taken down from the cross and laid in a grave.

Application. We should frequently think of Jesus crucified. Had He not died, we would have been eternally lost. So great was the Redeemer's love! So great is the value of our soul that the Son of God died to redeem it! We ought to give the crucifix the place of honor in our home.

RESURRECTION OF CHRIST

FIFTH ARTICLE OF THE CREED

He descended into hell, the third day He arose again from the dead

72. Where did the soul of Jesus go after death?

After death, the soul of Jesus descended into Limbo.

"Abraham's bosom" (Luke 16:22); "paradise" (Luke 23:43); "prison" (I Pet. 3:19).

73. What did Jesus do on the third day after His death?

On the third day after His death, Jesus reunited His soul to His body and arose gloriously from the dead.

Easter Sunday: first Sunday following the full moon after the spring equinox (March 21).

"This Jesus hath God raised again, whereof all we are witnesses" (Acts 2:32). "But now Christ is risen from the dead, the first fruits of them that sleep" (I Cor. 15:20).

Application. God alone could raise Himself from the dead to life. This is the greatest miracle and the strongest proof that Christ is God. As Christ rose from the dead, so we also shall rise on the last day, glorious and transfigured, if we have lived a good life.

ASCENSION OF CHRIST

SIXTH ARTICLE OF THE CREED

He ascended into heaven; sitteth at the right hand of God, the Father Almighty

74. What did Jesus do on the fortieth day after His resurrection?

On the fortieth day after His resurrection, Jesus ascended into heaven.

Feast of the Ascension, forty days after Easter. Mount Olivet.

75. What is meant by the words, "sitteth at the right hand of God, the Father Almighty"?

By the words, "sitteth at the right hand of God, the Father Almighty," is meant that Jesus, as man, occupies the place of honor in heaven.

76. What does Jesus do for us in heaven?

In heaven Jesus intercedes for us and prepares a dwelling place for us.

"We have an advocate with the Father, Jesus Christ" (I John 2:1).

"I go to prepare a place for you" (John 14:2).

Application. We should often raise our eyes and heart to heaven and say: There is my real home! Christ Himself has prepared a dwelling for me there. I will live so as not to lose it through my fault.

SECOND COMING OF CHRIST

SEVENTH ARTICLE OF THE CREED

From thence He shall come to judge the living and the dead

77. For what purpose will Jesus come to earth again?

Jesus will come to earth again to judge all men.

General judgment.

"This Jesus who is taken up from you into heaven, shall so come as you have seen Him going into heaven" (Acts 1:11).

78. What will happen immediately after Jesus has judged mankind?

Immediately after Jesus has judged mankind, the just with body and soul will enter heaven, and the wicked with body and soul will be cast into hell.

Doomsday. "Of that day and hour no one knoweth" (Matt. 24:36).

"Come, ye blessed of My Father, possess you the kingdom prepared for you from the foundation of the world" (Matt. 25:34).

"Depart from Me, you cursed, into everlasting fire, which was prepared for the devil and his angels" (Matt. 25:41).

Application. The same Savior who came into the world as a poor infant to redeem us, will come again with divine majesty to judge us. Let us follow the Redeemer, that He may one day be to us a merciful judge.

THE HOLY GHOST

EIGHTH ARTICLE OF THE CREED

I believe in the Holy Ghost

79. Who is the Holy Ghost?

The Holy Ghost is the third Person of the Blessed Trinity, equal to the Father and the Son.

80. When did Jesus send the Holy Ghost upon the Church?

Jesus sent the Holy Ghost upon the Church on Pentecost.

Pentecost=fiftieth day.

Feast of Pentecost, fifty days after Easter.

"And when the days of the Pentecost were accomplished, they were all together in one place.... And they were all filled with the Holy Ghost" (Acts 2:1, 4).

81. What does the Holy Ghost do?

The Holy Ghost:

1. inspired the Bible;
2. enlightens and guides the rulers of the Church;
3. sanctifies men through the sacraments.

"For prophecy came not by will of man at any time; but the holy men of God spoke, inspired by the Holy Ghost" (II Pet. 1:21).

"But when He, the Spirit of truth, is come, He will teach you all truth" (John 16:13).

"Know you not that you are the temple of God, and that the Spirit of God dwelleth in you?" (I Cor. 3:16.)

82. What does the Bible contain?

The Bible contains those revealed truths that were written by men chosen and inspired by the Holy Ghost.

Scripture=writing. Holy Writ. There are 72 books in the Bible.

Inspiration is a grace moving a man faithfully to write what God wishes written.

Each writing in the collection has two authors, the divine author (the Holy Spirit) and a human author.

The Church is the teacher; the Bible is her book.

A list of the books of the Bible will be found on page 102.

83. What does tradition contain?

Tradition contains those truths which were preached but not written by the apostles, and which were handed down in the Church from age to age.

"Many other signs also did Jesus in the sight of His disciples, which are not written in this book" (John 20:30).

"Hold the traditions which you have learned, whether by word or by our epistle" (II Thess. 2:15).

84. How long does the Holy Ghost dwell in the soul?

The Holy Ghost dwells in the soul as long as it is free from mortal sin.

"Know you not that your members are the temple of the Holy Ghost, who is in you, whom you have from God: and you are not your own?" (I Cor. 6:19.)

Application. All sanctity comes from the Holy Ghost. He sanctified us also by His grace, and made our soul His temple. Let us not drive Him from His temple by sin.

THE CHURCH

The Holy Catholic Church

85. Who belong to the Church?

Those belong to the Church, who are baptized, believe all that God has revealed, and are in union with the Pope of Rome.

86. Who founded the Church?

Jesus Christ founded the Church.

87. How did Jesus Christ found the Church?

Jesus Christ founded the Church by giving her the apostles as rulers and commanding all men to obey them.

Clergy and laity.

88. Whom did Jesus appoint as head of the Church?

Jesus appointed St. Peter as head of the Church.

89. What did Jesus say when He appointed St. Peter as head of the Church?

When appointing St. Peter as head of the Church, Jesus said: "Thou art Peter, and upon this rock I will build My Church, and the gates of hell shall not prevail against it" (Matt. 16:18).

"And I will give to thee the keys of the kingdom of heaven; and whatsoever thou shalt bind upon earth shall be bound also in heaven, and whatsoever thou shalt loose on earth it shall be loosed also in heaven" (Matt. 16:19).

"Feed My lambs, feed My sheep" (John 21:16-17).

90. Who is the successor of St. Peter?

The successor of St. Peter is the Pope, the Bishop of Rome.

Title: Holy Father; Vicar of Christ.

Who is the present Pope?

91. Who are the successors of the apostles?

The successors of the apostles are the bishops.

Archbishops, bishops, cardinals, diocese. Councils (ecumenical, provincial).

92. Who are the assistants of the bishops?

The assistants of the bishops are the priests.

93. Is the Church one?

The Church is one, for all Catholics have the same doctrine, and the same sacraments, and are under the same head.

The four marks of the true Church: unity, holiness, Catholicity and apostolicity.

94. Is the Church holy?

The Church is holy, for her doctrines, her precepts, and her sacraments are holy and make us holy.

95. Is the Church Catholic?

The Church is Catholic, for she was founded for all men and is spread over the whole world.

Catholic=universal.

96. Is the Church apostolic?

The Church is apostolic, for her doctrine and her rulers are from the apostles.

97. What do you mean by saying the Church is infallible?

By saying the Church is infallible we mean that she cannot err in matters of faith and morals.

"I am with you all days, even to the consummation of the world" (Matt. 28:20). "The Holy Ghost ... will teach you all things, and bring all things to your mind, whatsoever I shall have said to you" (John 14:26). The Church is "the pillar and ground of the truth" (I Tim. 3:15).

98. Is the Pope infallible?

The Pope is infallible, when he solemnly declares a truth which Catholics must believe.

99. How long will the Church last?

The Church will last till the end of the world; and her enemies cannot destroy it.

"The gates of hell shall not prevail against it" (Matt. 16:18).

100. Can anyone be saved who remains out of the Church through his own fault?

No one can be saved who remains out of the Church through his own fault.

There is but one true Church. It alone has power to save.

101. How can we help the Church to spread over the world?

We can help the Church to spread over the world:

1. by giving alms for the missionaries and missions;
2. by prayer.

A fervent Catholic belongs to a missionary society (Society for the Propagation of Faith, Holy Childhood Society, Sodality of St. Peter Claver) and reads missionary magazines.

Home missions; foreign missions.

102. Will all the members of the Church be saved?

Not all the members of the Church will be saved, but only those who practice their religion.

Practical Catholics. Not lax or nominal Catholics.

Excommunication.

"Not every one that saith to Me, Lord, Lord, shall enter into the kingdom of heaven; but he that doth the will of My Father in heaven, he shall enter into the kingdom of heaven" (Matt. 7:21).

Application. We should give thanks to God that we are members of the Catholic Church. If we live as good Catholics, we will die as such, and go to heaven. We ought to pray for the conversion of non-Catholics and take an active interest in Catholic Action and in mission work, both domestic and foreign.

THE COMMUNION OF SAINTS

103. Who belong to the communion of saints?

To the communion of saints belong:

1. the members of the Church on earth;
2. the souls in purgatory;
3. the saints in heaven.

Church militant, suffering, and triumphant.

104. In what does the communion of saints consist?

The communion of saints consists in this, that its members love and help one another.

105. How do the members of the Church help one another?

The members of the Church help one another by prayer and good works.

106. How do we help the poor souls in purgatory?

We help the poor souls in purgatory by prayer, good works, indulgences, and especially by the holy sacrifice of the Mass.

"It is a holy and a wholesome thought to pray for the dead, that they may be loosed from sins" (II Mach. 12:46).

All Souls Day, November 2.

107. How do the saints in heaven help us?

The saints in heaven help us by praying for us.

Application. All Christians are benefited by our good works, as we are benefited by theirs. Let us often pray for the poor souls; they are in great need of assistance. They are grateful for our prayers.

REMISSION OF SINS

TENTH ARTICLE OF THE CREED

Forgiveness of sins

108. How does God forgive us our sins?

God forgives us our sins by the sacraments of baptism and penance.

Application. What we need more than anything else is to get rid of our sins. Sin is the great obstacle to our salvation. We should be thankful to God that He has made provision in His Church for the remission of sins.

THE FOUR LAST THINGS

ELEVENTH AND TWELFTH ARTICLES OF THE CREED

The resurrection of the body; and life
everlasting.   Amen.

109. Which are the four last things of man?

The four last things of man are death, judgment,
heaven, and hell.

DEATH

110. What happens when a person dies?

When a person dies his soul separates from his body.

111. What is certain about our death?

It is certain that we must all die.

"By one man sin entered into this world, and by sin death"
(Rom. 5:12).

112. What is uncertain about our death?

It is uncertain when, where, and how we shall die.

"Wherefore be you also ready, because at what hour you know
not the Son of man will come" (Matt. 24:44).

JUDGMENT

**113. Where does the soul of man go immediately after
death?**

Immediately after death the soul of man goes before
the judgment seat of God.

"It is appointed unto men once to die, and after this the
judgment" (Heb. 9:27).

Particular judgment.

114. Where does the soul go after the particular judgment?

After the particular judgment, the soul goes to heaven, to hell, or to purgatory.

115. What souls go to heaven immediately?

Those souls go to heaven immediately that are free from sin and from the punishment due to sin.

116. What souls go to hell?

The souls of those who have died in mortal sin go to hell.

117. What souls go to purgatory?

Those souls go to purgatory that have yet to atone for venial sins, or to suffer the temporal punishment due to sin.

"There shall not enter into it anything defiled" (Apoc. 21:27).

118. How long must souls remain in purgatory?

Souls must remain in purgatory until they are free from sin and the punishment due to sin.

119. Will there be a purgatory after the general judgment?

After the general judgment there will be no purgatory: there will be only heaven and hell.

RESURRECTION

120. What will become of the body on the last day?

On the last day, God will restore the body from the dust and reunite it to the soul.

"The hour cometh wherein all that are in the graves shall hear the voice of the Son of God; and they that have done good things shall come forth unto the resurrection of life; but they that have done evil, unto the resurrection of judgment" (John 5:28, 29).

121. How will the risen bodies appear?

The risen bodies of the just will appear glorious and transfigured; the bodies of the wicked will appear hideous and loathsome.

"We shall all indeed rise again: but we shall not all be changed" (I Cor. 15:51).

HEAVEN

122. What is heaven?

Heaven is the place of everlasting happiness.

123. In what does the happiness of the blessed in heaven consist?

The happiness of the blessed in heaven consists chiefly in this, that for all eternity

1. they are free from all evils;
2. they see God;
3. they are united with Him in the most intimate love.

"Eye hath not seen nor ear heard, nor hath it entered into the heart of man, what things God hath prepared for them that love Him" (I Cor. 2:9).

124. Will the just be equally happy in heaven?

The just will not be equally happy in heaven: he who merited more, will receive a greater reward.

"He who soweth sparingly, shall also reap sparingly, and he who soweth in blessings, shall also reap blessings" (II Cor. 9:6).

HELL

125. What is hell?

Hell is the place of eternal torments.

126. In what do the torments of the damned consist?

The torments of the damned chiefly consist in this, that for all eternity

1. they enjoy no happiness;
2. they cannot see and love God;
3. they burn in everlasting fire.

"These shall go into everlasting punishment" (Matt. 25:46). "Where their worm dieth not, and the fire is not extinguished" (Mark 9:45).

127. Will the damned suffer equal pains?

The damned will not suffer equal pains; those who have sinned more, will also be punished more severely.

Application. "In all thy works remember thy last end, and thou shalt never sin" (Ecclus. 7:40). Let us often say to ourselves: I must die, and know not where or how or when. My body will decay; my soul is immortal. I will therefore take more care of my soul than of my body. I will save my soul, else I shall be lost eternally.

PART II

WE MUST KEEP THE COMMANDMENTS

The two fundamental laws: love God above all things;
love thy neighbor as thyself.

128. How should we love God?

We should love God above all things.

"Thou shalt love the Lord thy God with thy whole heart,
and with thy whole soul, and with thy whole mind, and with
thy whole strength" (Mark 12:30). "He that loveth father
or mother more than Me is not worthy of Me" (Matt. 10:37).

129. Why should we love God?

We should love God:

1. because He is infinitely good and perfect;
2. because He is our greatest benefactor.

"Let us therefore love God, because God first hath loved us"
(I John 4:19).

130. How do we show that we love God?

We show that we love God by doing His holy will.

"If any one love Me, he will keep My word" (John 14:23).

Application. No one can love God as much as He deserves
to be loved. Let us think of God every day and rather suffer
the loss of anything than be separated from God by mortal
sin.

LOVE OF OUR NEIGHBOR

131. Who is our neighbor?

Our neighbor is everybody without exception.

132. Why should we love all men?

We should love all men:

    1. because all men are God's children;

    2. because we are destined to be united in heaven.

133. How do we love our neighbor?

We love our neighbor by wishing him well and doing good to him when we can.

"All things whatsoever you would that men should do to you, do you also to them" (Matt. 7:12).

Corporal works of mercy	Spiritual works of mercy
1. to feed the hungry	1. to admonish the sinner
2. to give drink to the thirsty	2. to instruct the ignorant
3. to shelter the homeless	3. to counsel the doubtful
4. to clothe the naked	4. to comfort the sorrowful
5. to visit the sick	5. to bear wrongs patiently
6. to ransom captives	6. to forgive all injuries
7. to bury the dead	7. to pray for the living and the dead

(Matt. 25:35, 36).

Examples: St. Martin, St. Vincent de Paul, St. Elizabeth.

134. Why must we love our enemies?

We must love our enemies because Christ has expressly commanded it.

"Love your enemies, do good to them that hate you, and pray for them that persecute and calumniate you" (Matt. 5:44).

135. How do we show that we love our enemies?

We show that we love our enemies:

    1. by forgiving them from our hearts;

    2. by assisting them in need;

    3. by praying for them.

"If you will not forgive, neither will your Father that is in heaven forgive you your sins" (Mark 11:26).

Examples: Jesus on the cross; St. Stephen.

Parable: the good Samaritan (Luke 10:30-37).

Application. We cannot love God unless we love our neighbor. We should be kind to everyone and observe the golden rule. We know that Christ looks upon kindness done to our neighbor as if done to Him (Matt. 25:40). We should contribute cheerfully to Catholic charities, such as orphanages, hospitals, homes for the aged.

THE TEN COMMANDMENTS OF GOD

136. Recite the Ten Commandments.

1. I am the Lord thy God. Thou shalt not have strange gods before Me; thou shalt not make to thyself any graven thing to adore it.
2. Thou shalt not take the name of the Lord thy God in vain.
3. Remember that thou keep holy the Sabbath day.
4. Honor thy father and thy mother, that it may be well with thee, and thou mayest live long on the earth.
5. Thou shalt not kill.
6. Thou shalt not commit adultery.
7. Thou shalt not steal.
8. Thou shalt not bear false witness against thy neighbor.
9. Thou shalt not covet thy neighbor's wife.
10. Thou shalt not covet thy neighbor's goods.

(Ex. 20:1-17.)

Decalogue.

FIRST COMMANDMENT

Thou shalt adore the Lord thy God

137. To what does the first commandment oblige us?

The first commandment obliges us to believe in God, to hope in Him, to love Him, and to adore Him.

FAITH

138. Is it enough to believe in God in our hearts only?

It is not enough to believe in God in our hearts only; we must also show our faith outwardly.

"Everyone therefore that shall confess Me before men, I will also confess him before My Father who is in heaven" (Matt. 10:32).

139. How do we show our faith outwardly?

We show our faith outwardly:

1. by saying that we are Catholics;
2. by doing what our faith teaches.

"Let your light shine before men, that they may see your good works and glorify your Father who is in heaven" (Matt. 5:16).

140. How do we sin against faith?

We sin against faith:

1. by wilfully doubting in matters of faith;
2. by denying the faith;
3. by speaking against faith;
4. by given up the faith.

141. Which are the chief causes that lead to loss of faith?

The chief causes that lead to loss of faith are:
1. lack of religious instruction;
2. leading a bad life;
3. mixed marriages;
4. reading of bad books and magazines.

HOPE

142. What is meant by hope in God?

Hope in God means trusting firmly that He will give us all that He has promised.

143. What has God promised us?

God has promised:
1. to pardon our sins;
2. to give us the necessary graces;
3. to hear our prayers;
4. to take us to heaven.

144. Why should we firmly hope in God?

We should firmly hope in God because He is almighty, good, and faithful.

145. When do we sin against hope?

We sin against hope when we:
1. do not hope at all (despair);
2. do not hope firmly (distrust);
3. hope too much (presumption);
4. hope superstitiously (superstition).

146. Who hopes superstitiously?

He hopes superstitiously who attributes to anything a secret power which God has not given it.

Four forms of superstition:
1. fortune telling: trying to discover the future;
2. vain observance: trying to obtain things by magic or charm;
3. spiritism: pretended calling-up of the dead;
4. Christian Science: pretending to repeat Christ's miracles of healing.

LOVE

147. How do we fail against the love of God?

We fail against the love of God by every sin that we commit.

ADORATION

148. What is meant by the words "to adore God"?

"To adore God" means to give Him the highest honor, because He is the Lord of all things.

"The Lord thy God shalt thou adore, and Him only shalt thou serve" (Matt. 4:10).

149. How do we adore God outwardly?

We adore God outwardly:
1. by taking part in divine service;
2. by receiving the sacraments;
3. by reciting vocal prayers.

150. How do we sin against the worship which we owe God?

We sin against the worship which we owe God:
1. by neglecting Mass, sacraments, and prayer;
2. by taking part in worship not approved by the Church;
3. by committing sacrilege.

Idolatry.

151. Who commits a sacrilege?

He commits a sacrilege who makes a bad use of a sacred thing.

Sacred persons: priests.
Sacred things: sacraments, chalice, crucifix.
Sacred places: church, cemetery.

Application. We should make acts of faith, hope, and charity every day. We must safeguard our faith, and shun whatever is dangerous to it. If we lose our faith, all is lost. In all necessities of soul and body let us place our confidence in God. Let us never use forbidden or superstitious means to cure disease, to obtain riches, or to discover hidden things. We should not circulate "chain prayers."

VENERATION OF THE SAINTS

152. Why does it please God if we honor the saints?

It pleases God if we honor the saints because they are His special friends.

153. How do we honor the saints?

We honor the saints:
1. by asking them to intercede for us;
2. by showing respect to their relics and images;
3. by imitating their example.

154. Why do we honor sacred images?

We honor sacred images because we thereby show respect to Christ Himself and His saints.

Crucifix=cross with image of Christ on it.

155. Why do we honor the Blessed Virgin Mary in a special manner?

We honor the Blessed Virgin Mary in a special manner:

1. because she is the Mother of God;
2. because she is also our mother;
3. because she is the Queen of all the angels and saints;
4. because her intercession is very powerful.

"Behold from henceforth all generations shall call me blessed" (Luke 1:48).

Prayers: Hail Mary, rosary, litany, Memorare.

Hymns: Salve Regina, Regina coeli laetare.

Shrines: Loreto, Lourdes.

Articles: medal, scapular.

Application. It is useful to pray to the saints. Let us have confidence in Mary, our heavenly mother. We should strive to become holy like the saints.

SECOND COMMANDMENT

Thou shalt not take the name of the Lord thy God in vain

156. How do we dishonor the name of God?

We dishonor the name of God:

1. by pronouncing it irreverently;
2. by cursing;
3. by blaspheming;
4. by sinful swearing;
5. by not keeping a vow.

157. What is cursing?

Cursing is calling evil down on someone.

Opposite of blessing.

158. What is blaspheming?

Blaspheming is speaking impiously of God, of His saints, or of holy things.

159. What is swearing?

Swearing is calling God to witness that we speak the truth.

Oath.

160. When is swearing sinful?

Swearing is sinful:

    1. when we swear falsely (perjury);

    2. when we swear without necessity;

    3. when we swear to do evil.

161. What kind of sin is it to swear falsely?

It is a very grievous sin against God and man to swear falsely.

"Thus saith the Lord of hosts: it (the curse) shall come to the house of him that sweareth falsely by My name; and it shall remain in the midst of his house, and shall consume it, with the timbers and the stones thereof" (Zach. 5:4).

162. What is a vow?

A vow is a promise made to God to do a good deed with the intention of binding oneself under the pain of sin.

163. When do we sin against a vow?

We sin against a vow when, through our own fault, we do not keep what we have promised to God.

"If thou hast vowed anything to God, defer not to pay it, for an unfaithful and foolish promise displeaseth Him; but whatsoever thou hast vowed, pay it. And it is much better not to vow, than after a vow not to perform the thing promised" (Eccles. 5:3, 4).

Application. Cursing is the language of the reprobates in hell. If we are called upon in court to take an oath, we should do so reverently. Let us never use sacred names to express surprise or anger. We should not vow anything important without first consulting the priest.

THIRD COMMANDMENT

Remember that thou keep holy the Sabbath day

164. Which is the Lord's Day?

Sunday, the first day of the week, is the Lord's Day.

165. Which days must we observe like Sunday?

We must observe the holydays of obligation like Sunday.

166. Which are the holydays of obligation in the United States?

The holydays of obligation in the United States are:
1. the Immaculate Conception, December 8.
2. Christmas, December 25.
3. the Circumcision of our Lord, January 1.
4. the Ascension of Christ, forty days after Easter.
5. the Assumption of the Blessed Virgin, August 15.
6. All Saints Day, November 1.

167. How must we keep the Sundays and holydays of obligation?

We must keep the Sundays and holydays of obligation:

    1. by not doing servile work;

    2. by attending Mass.

"Six days shalt thou labor, and shalt do all thy works. The seventh is the day of the Sabbath, that is, the rest of the Lord thy God. Thou shalt not do any work therein" (Deut. 5:13, 14).

Application. If we desire God's blessing, we must observe the Sunday. Neglecting Mass is a step towards apostasy. We should not do unnecessary servile work. We should accept no job in which we will be unable to observe the Sunday.

FOURTH COMMANDMENT

Thou shalt honor thy father and thy mother

168. Why must children honor their parents?

Children must honor their parents:

    1. because father and mother take the place of God in their regard;

    2. because, next to God, their parents are their greatest benefactors.

169. How do children honor their parents?

Children honor their parents:

    1. by loving them;

    2. by obeying them;

    3. by praying for them.

Sins against the fourth commandment: see page 100.

170. What may obedient children expect in this life?

Obedient children may expect God's blessing in this life.

"Honor thy father and thy mother, which is the first commandment with a promise, that it may be well with thee, and thou mayest be long-lived upon earth" (Ephes. 6:2, 3).

171. What may disobedient children expect in this life?

Disobedient children may expect God's curse and the contempt of all good people in this life.

"Cursed be he that honoreth not his father and mother; and all the people shall say: Amen" (Deut. 27:16).

Examples: Cham, Absalom, the sons of Heli.

172. Must we obey only our parents?

We must obey not only our parents, but also all other superiors.

Spiritual superiors: pope, bishop, pastor, confessor.

Secular superiors: president, governor, municipal authorities, parents, teachers, guardians, employers.

173. Why must we obey our superiors?

We must obey our superiors because they have their authority from God.

"Let every soul be subject to higher powers: for there is no power but from God, and those that are, are ordained of God" (Rom. 13:1). "Servants, obey in all things your masters according to the flesh; not serving to the eye as pleasing men, but in simplicity of heart, fearing God" (Col. 3:22).

174. When are parents and superiors not to be obeyed?

Parents and superiors are not to be obeyed when they command anything sinful.

"We ought to obey God rather than men" (Acts 5:29).

175. Whom should we, as Christians, especially honor?

As Christians we should especially honor the pope, bishop, and pastor.

"With all thy soul fear the Lord, and reverence His priests" (Ecclus. 7:31). "He that heareth you, heareth Me; and he that despiseth you, despiseth Me" (Luke 10:16).

Application. God makes His own will known to us through our superiors. Therefore we should respect all rightful superiors. There can be no order and peace in the home or in the country without submission to authority. Let us love God, our home, and our country.

FIFTH COMMANDMENT

Thou shalt not kill

176. Who is the Lord and owner of our life?

God alone is the Lord and owner of our life.

177. How do we sin against our own life?

We sin against our own life:
1. if we take our life (suicide);
2. if we endanger our life rashly;
3. if we injure our health.

The Church refuses burial to those who commit suicide, unless they were out of their mind.

Health is injured by premature and excessive use of tobacco, by intemperance in the drinking of intoxicants and in eating.

178. How do we sin against the life of our neighbor?

We sin against the life of our neighbor:

1. if we take his life (murder);
2. if we shorten his life;
3. if we strike or wound him.

To take human life is lawful only:

1. for the civil authority in punishing criminals;
2. in war;
3. in self-defense.

Adulterated food and harsh treatment are injurious. Violation of traffic regulations is often dangerous.

179. How do we injure the soul of our neighbor?

We injure the soul of our neighbor by giving scandal.

180. What is meant by giving scandal?

By giving scandal is meant the leading of others into sin.

"But he that shall scandalize one of these little ones that believe in Me, it were better for him that a millstone should be hanged about his neck and that he should be drowned in the depth of the sea ... . Woe to that man by whom the scandal cometh" (Matt. 18:6, 7).

Nine ways of being accessory to the sins of another: by counsel, command, consent, provocation, praise or flattery, concealment, partaking, silence, defense of the evil done.

181. How do we sin in thought against the fifth commandment?

We sin in thought against the fifth commandment if we hate, envy, or wish evil to our neighbor.

"Whosoever hateth his brother is a murderer" (I John 3:15). Quarreling, insults.

Application. Life and health are great blessings. We must avoid injuring our neighbor in his life or health. When driving an automobile, we should obey the traffic laws. Everyone ought to take reasonable care of his health so that he may serve God better and longer. More precious than the life of the body is the supernatural life of the soul, that is, sanctifying grace.

SIXTH AND NINTH COMMANDMENTS

Thou shalt not commit adultery
Thou shalt not covet thy neighbor's wife

182. Which is the most beautiful virtue?

The most beautiful virtue is purity.

Chastity, modesty, decency.

"O how beautiful is the chaste generation with glory; for the memory thereof is immortal, because it is known both to God and men" (Wis. 4:1).

183. How do we sin against purity?

We sin against purity by taking wilful pleasure in impure things.

Impure thoughts, desires, talk, looks, reading, actions.

Impurity, unchastity, lust, immorality, voluptuousness.

184. Why must we shun impurity?

We must shun impurity:

1. because no sin is more shameful;
2. because it has such evil consequences for soul and body.

"They shall have their portion in the pool burning with fire and brimstone, which is the second death" (Apoc. 21:8).

Examples: The Deluge, Sodom and Gomorrha.

Impurity destroys innocence, makes a person unfit for mental work, ruins the health, plunges into disgrace, causes despondency, and even leads to suicide.

185. What are the things that often lead to impurity?

The things that often lead to impurity are:
1. familiarity with persons of the other sex;
2. bad companions, drinking, idleness;
3. curiosity, sexy magazines;
4. indecent dress, movies, and dances.

186. What should we do to preserve chastity?

To preserve chastity we should:
1. shun what leads to impurity;
2. receive the sacraments often;
3. honor the Blessed Virgin Mary.

"Every one of you should know how to possess his vessel in sanctification and honor" (I Thess. 4:4).

Application. Innocence makes us like the angels and leads us to heaven. Familiarity with persons of the other sex may lead to impurity. Immodest magazines ruin soul and mind. Let us often recall the words of our divine Savior: "Blessed are the clean of heart, for they shall see God" (Matt. 5:8).

SEVENTH AND TENTH COMMANDMENTS

Thou shalt not steal
Thou shalt not covet thy neighbor's goods

187. Who gave man the right to own things?

God gave man the right to own things.

"And God blessed them, saying: Increase and multiply, and fill the earth, and subdue it, and rule over the fishes of the sea, and the fowls of the air, and all living creatures that move upon the earth" (Gen. 1:28).

God, as Creator, is the owner of all things. We have to render an account to Him for the way in which we use His things.

Labor, contract (buying), donation, and inheritance are some of the ways of acquiring property.

Socialists, communists.

188. How do we injure our neighbor in his property?

We injure our neighbor in his property:

1. by stealing;
2. by cheating;
3. by not restoring things found;
4. by not paying debts;
5. by damaging his property.

Theft, robbery, fraud, forgery, embezzling, counterfeiting money, picking pockets, shoplifting, arson, graft, receiving or buying stolen goods, usury, dishonest labor, insufficient wages.

It is impossible to enumerate the many ways of being dishonest.

189. What must we do when we have injured our neighbor in his property?

When we have injured our neighbor in his property, we must repair the injury.

Restitution. We must restore as fully as possible the ill-gotten goods or their value as soon as we are able; to the owner or to his heirs. If several have conspired to steal, one must restore all, if the others are unwilling to do their share.

He who is not willing to make restitution remains in sin and cannot be forgiven.

190. When do we covet our neighbor's goods?

We covet our neighbor's goods when we wish to acquire them in an unlawful manner.

"The desire of money is the root of all evils" (I Tim. 6:10).

Application. We may rightly strive by diligence and thrift to increase our possessions. But we must give to every one whatever is his and never take what does not belong to us, however trifling. Whoever steals little things may end by stealing big things. We should avoid gambling, beware of avarice, and do our work conscientiously.

EIGHTH COMMANDMENT

Thou shalt not bear false witness against thy neighbor

191. How do we sin against the eighth commandment?

We sin against the eighth commandment:
1. if we tell a lie;
2. if we rob our neighbor of his good name.

192. What is meant by lying?

By lying is meant saying what is not true with the intention of deceiving.

"You are of your father the devil" (John 8:44).
"Lying lips are an abomination to the Lord" (Prov. 12:22).
Hypocrisy=pretending to be better than we are.

193. How do we rob our neighbor of his good name?

We rob our neighbor of his good name:
1. by thinking evil of him without a good reason (false suspicion);
2. by telling his hidden faults without necessity (detraction);
3. by falsely accusing him of something bad (slander).

"Judge not, and you shall not be judged" (Luke 6:37).
Gossiping, talebearing.

194. What is he obliged to do, who by slander has injured his neighbor's reputation?

He who by slander has injured his neigbor's reputation must retract the slander and repair the injury.

Application. We should never tell a lie or act the hypocrite. We should speak kindly of others. A good reputation is more precious than riches. We ought not willingly listen to detraction or slander. "He who speaks such things has the devil in his mouth; he who listens to them, has the devil in his ear" (St. Bernard).

THE PRECEPTS OF THE CHURCH

195. Which are the chief precepts of the Church?

The chief precepts of the Church are:

1. to attend Mass on Sundays and holydays of obligation;
2. to fast and abstain on the days appointed;
3. to confess at least once a year and to receive the Holy Eucharist during the Easter period;
4. not to join forbidden societies;
5. to contribute to the support of the Church;
6. to give children a religious education;
7. not to marry contrary to the laws of the Church.

Canon law=collection of the precepts of the Church.

196. From whom has the Church received the right to make precepts for her members?

The Church has received the right to make precepts for her members from Jesus Christ.

"Whatsoever you shall bind upon earth, shall be bound also in heaven; and whatsoever you shall loose upon earth, shall be loosed also in heaven" (Matt. 18:18).

"He that heareth you, heareth Me; and he that despiseth you, despiseth Me; and he that despiseth Me, despiseth Him that sent Me" (Luke 10:16).

"If he will not hear the Church, let him be to thee as the heathen and publican" (Matt. 18:17).

FIRST PRECEPT OF THE CHURCH

To attend Mass on Sundays and holydays of obligation

197. Who is obliged to attend Mass on Sundays and holydays of obligation?

Every Catholic who has come to the use of reason is obliged to attend Mass on Sundays and holydays of obligation.

SECOND PRECEPT OF THE CHURCH

To fast and abstain on the days appointed

198. What is meant by fasting?

By fasting is meant taking but one full meal a day. From the age of 21 to 59.

199. Which are the days of fasting?

The days of fasting are:
1. Ash Wednesday
2. Good Friday.*

*This question has been changed in this printing to reflect the current rules.

200. What is meant by abstinence?

By abstinence is meant eating no meat.

From the age of seven.

201. Which are the days of abstinence in the United States?

The days of complete abstinence are:

1. All Fridays of Lent
2. Ash Wednesday and Good Friday.*

THIRD PRECEPT OF THE CHURCH

To confess at least once a year, and to receive the Holy Eucharist during the Easter period

202. How long does the Easter period last in the United States?

In the United States the Easter period lasts from the first Sunday in Lent until Trinity Sunday inclusive.

203. How long does the Easter duty bind?

The Easter duty binds even after the time has elapsed, until the duty is fulfilled.

*This question has been changed in this printing to reflect the current rules.

204. In the third precept, what do the words "at least" indicate?

In the third precept, the words "at least" indicate that all should receive the sacraments frequently.

He who has committed a mortal sin is obliged to receive the sacrament of penance.

We must receive the Holy Eucharist during the Easter period and as a preparation for death. We may receive the Holy Eucharist once a day. The Church urges us to receive this sacrament frequently.

FOURTH PRECEPT OF THE CHURCH

Not to join forbidden societies

205. What are forbidden societies?

Forbidden societies are:

1. those which conspire against the Church or the civil government;

2. those whose members take the oath of blind obedience or absolute secrecy;

3. those which have a ceremonial of their own not sanctioned by the Church.

A Catholic who joins the Freemasons is excommunicated from the Church.

Application. Under no condition may one become a member of a forbidden society or lodge. Membership in good, Catholic societies will be of great profit to us.

FIFTH PRECEPT OF THE CHURCH

To contribute to the support of the Church

206. Why must we contribute to the support of the Church?

We must contribute to the support of the Church because otherwise the Church cannot subsist.

"The laborer is worthy of his hire" (Luke 10:7). "The Lord ordained that they who preach the gospel should live by the gospel" (I Cor. 9:14).

The parochial school is a part of the parish.

207. Who is obliged to contribute to the support of the Church?

Every Catholic who is able to do so is obliged to contribute to the support of the Church.

Application. We should not be stingy toward God and His Church. We should cooperate with our pastor when he proposes needed improvements; we are the ones who benefit. If our parish has not sufficient revenue, the holding of divine services becomes difficult or impossible. Let us take pride in our parish church and school.

SIXTH PRECEPT OF THE CHURCH

To give children a religious education

208. Why must parents send their children to a Catholic school?

Parents must send their children to a Catholic school because without religious instruction they may lose their faith.

Only the bishop, after investigating the circumstances, may give permission for a child to be sent to a non-Catholic school. Parents who send a child to a non-Catholic school without a good reason may be refused the sacraments.

Application. Religion is the greatest thing in life. Education without it is incomplete. Children were created by God to serve Him. They cannot do so unless they are well instructed in Christian doctrine and trained in religious practice. Good parents have at heart the spiritual welfare of their children no less than their temporal welfare. They have to render an account to God for the way they brought up their children. "After the grace of baptism, the greatest grace in the world is that of Christian education" (Pius XI).

SEVENTH PRECEPT OF THE CHURCH

Not to marry contrary to the laws of the Church

209. What does the Church forbid those who intend to marry?

The Church forbids those who intend to marry
1. to marry a relative;
2. to marry a non-Catholic;
3. to marry without the three publications of the banns;
4. to marry before anyone but the pastor or his delegate.

210. Why does the Church abhor and forbid mixed marriages?

The Church abhors and forbids mixed marriages
1. because there is no true unity in them;
2. because the Catholic is in danger of losing the faith;
3. because the children usually are not brought up as good Catholics.

211. When should marriages not be solemnized?

Marriages should not be solemnized in Advent and Lent.

A Catholic who is not married before a priest and two witnesses is not validly married. For persons who live far away from any priest, the Church law makes special provision. A Catholic who is married before a minister is excommunicated.

Application. Anyone about to marry should see his pastor at least a month ahead of time.

SIN

212. How do we know what is good or bad?

We know what is good or bad by our conscience.

213. Who commits sin?

He commits sin who knowingly and wilfully does what God has forbidden.

Three requisites: to do what is bad; to know that it is bad; to intend to do it.

214. In how many ways can we sin?

We can sin by thoughts, desires, words, actions, and omissions.

215. Who commits grievous sin?

He commits grievous sin who sins in a matter that he knows is important.

216. Why are grievous sins called mortal sins?

Grievous sins are called mortal sins because they rob the soul of the life of grace.

"Thou hast the name of being alive, and thou art dead" (Apoc. 3:1). "All iniquity is sin. And there is a sin unto death" (I John 5:17).

217. Why is mortal sin the greatest evil?

Mortal sin is the greatest evil because it makes us an enemy of God.

"They who do such things shall not obtain the kingdom of God" (Gal. 5:21).

218. What do we lose by mortal sin?

By mortal sin we lose
1. sanctifying grace
2. heaven
3. all our merits.

219. Who commits a venial sin?

He commits a venial sin who sins in a matter that he knows is less important.

220. Why should we avoid also venial sin?

We should avoid also venial sin
1. because it offends God;
2. because it brings temporal punishment upon us;
3. because it gradually leads to mortal sin.

221. What generally leads us into sin?

Temptations and occasions generally lead us into sin.

222. What are temptations?

Temptations are suggestions to commit sin.

223. Where do temptations come from?

Temptations come from the devil, from wicked fellowmen, and from our own evil inclination.

224. When do temptations become sinful?

Temptations become sinful when we consent to them.

225. How must we resist temptations?

We must resist temptations by prayer and by driving them out of our mind.

"Watch ye, and pray that ye enter not into temptation" (Matt. 26:41).

226. What are sinful occasions?

Sinful occasions are persons, places, or things that easily lead us into sin.

Bad companions, public dances, filthy magazines, disreputable taverns.

227. What must we do when we happen to be in the occasion of sin?

When we are in the occasion of sin we must leave it as soon as we can.

"He that loveth danger shall perish in it" (Ecclus. 3:27).

VICE

228. What is vice?

Vice is the habit of committing mortal sin.

229. Which are the principal vices?

The principal vices are: pride, avarice, lust, envy, gluttony, anger, and sloth.

Capital sins. Deadly sins. Root sins.

230. When do we sin by pride?

We sin by pride when we think ourselves better than others and wish to be honored more than we deserve.

"God resisteth the proud, and giveth grace to the humble" (Jas. 4:6). Vanity, haughtiness.

231. When do we sin by avarice?

We sin by avarice when we love money too much and give little or nothing for good purposes.

"But they that will become rich fall into temptation ... For the desire of money is the root of all evils" (I Tim. 6:9,10).

232. When do we sin by lust?

We sin by lust when we indulge in impure thoughts, conversations, reading, or actions.

233. When do we sin by envy?

We sin by envy when we grieve at the good fortune of others and rejoice at their misfortune.

234. When do we sin by gluttony?

We sin by gluttony when we eat or drink too much or too greedily.

Drunkenness.

235. When do we sin by anger?

We sin by anger when we show our temper without a good reason or seek revenge.

"The anger of man worketh not the justice of God" (Jas. 1:20).

236. When do we sin by sloth?

We sin by sloth when we shun work and neglect our duties.

"Idleness hath taught much evil" (Ecclus. 33:29). "If any man will not work, neither let him eat" (II Thess. 3:10).

GOOD WORKS; VIRTUE; CHRISTIAN PERFECTION

237. When do our good works earn a heavenly reward?

Our good works earn a heavenly reward when we do them in the state of grace and with a good intention.

"Prayer is good, with fasting and alms, more than to lay up treasures of gold" (Tob. 12:8).

238. What do we gain by each meritorious work?

By each meritorious work we gain more grace on earth and more reward in heaven.

"Every man shall receive his own reward according to his own labor" (I Cor. 3:8).

239. When is our intention good?

Our intention is good when we perform our deeds out of obedience to God's will.

"Take heed that you do not your justice before men, to be seen by them; otherwise you shall not have a reward of your Father who is in heaven" (Matt. 6:1).

"All for Thee, O Jesus!" Morning offering.

240. Who is virtuous?

He is virtuous who is always striving and ready to do what is pleasing to God.

241. Which are the three divine virtues?

The three divine virtues are: faith, hope, and charity.

"Now there remain faith, hope, and charity, these three; but the greatest of these is charity" (I Cor. 13:13).

242. Which are some of the moral virtues?

Some of the moral virtues are:
1. humility
1. generosity
3. chastity
4. kindness
5. temperance
6. meekness
7. diligence
8. patience
9. honesty
10. obedience
11. truthfulness

243. Which are the evangelical counsels?

The evangelical counsels are:
1. voluntary poverty
2. perpetual chastity
3. obedience to a spiritual superior.

"If thou wilt enter into life, keep the commandments.... If thou wilt be perfect, go, sell what thou hast, and give to the poor, and thou shalt have treasure in heaven" (Matt. 19:17, 21).

244. Who are obliged to keep the evangelical counsels?

All those are obliged to keep the evangelical counsels who have bound themselves by a vow to do so.

Monks, nuns, sisters.

Application. We should bear in mind the following advice. Avoid mortal sin as it is the greatest evil. Keep out of the proximate occasion of sin. Banish bad thoughts immediately. Beware of getting the habit of committing any mortal sin. Keep in the state of grace so that your good deeds will be meritorious. Strive to acquire good habits. If you lead a devout life, you will have much peace of mind and will have a happy death and will attain to heaven.

GRACE

245. What do we need to keep the commandments?

To keep the commandments we need grace.

"Without Me you can do nothing" (John 15:5).

246. What is grace?

Grace is a gift that God confers upon our soul for our salvation.

"I am the vine, you the branches. He that abideth in Me, and I in him, the same beareth much fruit" (John 15:5).

247. What does actual grace do for us?

Actual grace enlightens our understanding and moves our will to do good and to avoid evil.

"We helping do exhort you, that you receive not the grace of God in vain" (II Cor. 6:1).

248. How do we specially obtain actual grace?

We specially obtain actual grace by the sacraments and prayer.

249. What does sanctifying grace do for us?

Sanctifying grace makes us holy and children of God.

"Behold what manner of charity the Father hath bestowed upon us, that we should be called and should be the sons of God" (I John 3:1).

250. How do we obtain sanctifying grace for the first time?

We obtain sanctifying grace for the first time in baptism.

251. How do we lose sanctifying grace?

We lose sanctifying grace by mortal sin.

"He that loveth not, abideth in death" (I John 3:14).

252. How do we regain sanctifying grace?

We regain sanctifying grace
1. by the sacrament of penance,
2. by an act of perfect contrition.

Application. Grace is of greater value than money, health, and life. To obtain this grace for us, Christ died on the cross. Only he who dies in the state of sanctifying grace can enter heaven. The more sanctifying grace we possess, the greater will be our happiness in heaven.

PART III

THE SACRAMENTS

253. What is a sacrament?

A sacrament is a visible sign which imparts grace to our soul.

254. Who instituted the sacraments?

Jesus Christ instituted the sacraments.

Ceremonies are supplied by the Church to edify and to add solemnity.

255. Which are the seven sacraments?

The seven sacraments are:

1. Baptism
2. Confirmation
3. Holy Eucharist
4. Penance
5. Extreme Unction
6. Holy Orders
7. Matrimony.

256. What sacraments can be received only once?

Baptism, confirmation, and holy orders can be received only once.

Indelible mark.

257. How must we receive the sacraments?

We must receive the sacraments worthily.

Unworthy reception is a sacrilege.

258. Which is the greatest sacrament?

The Holy Eucharist is the greatest sacrament.

259. Which is the most necessary sacrament?

Baptism is the most necessary sacrament.

Application. The sacraments are the most precious things on earth. We should have the greatest respect for them, and honor the priest who administers them to us. He is called "Father" because he imparts spiritual life into our souls through the sacraments. We should never profane a sacrament by receiving it unworthily.

BAPTISM

260. Why is baptism the most necessary sacrament?

Baptism is the most necessary sacrament

1. because without baptism no one can be saved;
2. because without baptism no other sacrament can be received.

"Unless a man be born again of water and the Holy Ghost, he cannot enter into the kingdom of God" (John 3:5).

Substitutes for the sacrament of baptism when the latter is impossible:

Baptism of desire: love of God, perfect contrition for sin, which include the desire to receive baptism.

Baptism of blood: suffering martyrdom for the sake of Christ before baptism can be received.

261. How is baptism administered?

Baptism is administered by pouring water on the head of the person to be baptized, and at the same time saying: "I baptize thee in the name of the Father, and of the Son, and of the Holy Ghost."

Any natural water. Enough to touch and flow on the skin.

"Going therefore, teach ye all nations, baptizing them in the name of the Father, and of the Son, and of the Holy Ghost" (Matt. 28:19).

262. What takes place in the soul of the person baptized?

The soul of the person baptized is cleansed from all sin and is sanctified by the grace of God.

Effects of baptism: it takes away original sin, all sins committed before baptism, the eternal punishment, all temporal punishment. It gives sanctifying grace, makes us adopted children of God, heirs of heaven, members of the Catholic Church; it infuses faith, hope, and charity, and imprints an indelible mark.

263. Who can baptize validly?

Anyone can baptize validly.

"Private" baptism.

264. Who has the right to baptize?

The pastor has the right to baptize.

265. When should children be baptized?

Children should, if possible, be baptized within one week after birth.

266. What must the sponsor do?

The sponsors must answer for the child at baptism and must later take care that he is brought up a Catholic.

267. Who can be a sponsor?

Only a practical Catholic, who is at least fourteen years old, can be a sponsor.

Ceremonies of Baptism

The name of a saint should be selected. See calendar on page 113.

Before baptism: exorcism, ephpheta, baptismal "vows," anointing with oil of catechumens, profession of faith.

After baptism: anointing with chrism, handing of white garment and lighted candle. Entry in the baptismal record.

Application. All our life let us thank God for our baptism. If we had not been baptized, we would not be a child of God and could not be saved. Out of gratitude, we ought to help others to be baptized, especially pagan children, through the Holy Childhood Society.

CONFIRMATION

268. Who administers confirmation?

The bishop administers confirmation.

"Now when the apostles, who were in Jerusalem, had heard that Samaria had received the word of God, they sent unto them Peter and John. Who, when they were come, prayed for them, that they might receive the Holy Ghost. For He was not as yet come upon any of them, but they were only baptized in the name of the Lord Jesus. Then they laid their hands upon them, and they received the Holy Ghost" (Acts 8:14-17).

269. How does the bishop administer confirmation?

The bishop administers confirmation by placing his hand on the head of the person to be confirmed and anointing the forehead with chrism, in the form of a cross, saying: "I sign thee with the sign of the cross, and I confirm thee with the chrism of salvation, in the name of the Father; and of the Son, and of the Holy Ghost."

The one confirmed answers: "Amen."

Chrism is a mixture of olive oil and balsam, blessed by the bishop on Holy Thursday.

270. What takes place in the soul of the person confirmed?

The soul of the person confirmed receives the gifts of the Holy Ghost and is strengthened in the faith.

The seven gifts of the Holy Ghost: wisdom, understanding, counsel, fortitude, knowledge, piety, fear of the Lord. (Is. 11:2).

Neglect to receive confirmation is a sin.

271. What should we do before confirmation?

Before confirmation we should
1. attend the confirmation class;
2. pray earnestly to the Holy Ghost (novena);
3. make a good confession.

Application. Everyone should prepare well for confirmation. It can be received only once. When we have received it we are no longer children in the sight of the Church. We are then soldiers of Jesus Christ. We ought to profess and practice our faith manfully. We should not expel the Holy Ghost by mortal sin.

THE HOLY EUCHARIST

1. THE SACRAMENT

272. What is the Holy Eucharist?

The Holy Eucharist is the body and blood of our Lord Jesus Christ under the appearances of bread and wine.

Other names: Blessed Sacrament of the Altar, Lord's Supper, Corpus Christi, Sacred Host, Bread of Angels, Heavenly Manna, Viaticum (food for a journey).

273. How is Jesus Christ present in the Holy Eucharist?

Jesus Christ is present in the Holy Eucharist as He is in heaven.

Jesus is present really; not figuratively, not in a symbol. He is present truly; not imagined, not in a picture. He is present essentially, as God and as man.

274. When did Jesus promise the Blessed Sacrament?

Jesus promised the Blessed Sacrament after the miracle of the loaves and fishes.

"The bread that I will give is My flesh for the life of the world. ... Amen, amen I say unto you: Except you eat the flesh of the Son of man, and drink His blood, you shall not have life in you .... For My flesh is meat indeed, and My blood is drink indeed" (John 6:52, 54). Read John 6:25-70.

275. When did Jesus institute the Blessed Sacrament?

Jesus instituted the Blessed Sacrament on the eve of His death.

Holy Thursday.

276. How did Jesus institute the Blessed Sacrament?

Jesus took bread, blessed it, broke it, and gave it to His disciples, saying: "Take ye, and eat; this is My body." He then took the chalice with wine, blessed it, and gave it to His disciples, saying: "Drink ye all of this; for this is My blood. ... Do this for a commemoration of Me."

277. What happened when Jesus said, "This is My body," "this is My blood"?

When Jesus said, "This is My body," "this is My blood," the bread was changed into His body, and the wine into His blood.

Transubstantiation=change of a thing into something else.

278. What power did Jesus give to His apostles when He said, "Do this for a commemoration of Me"?

When Jesus said, "Do this for a commemoration of Me," He gave to His apostles the power to change bread and wine into His body and blood.

The apostles were the first Catholic priests.

279. Who received from the apostles the power of changing bread and wine into the body and blood of Christ?

The bishops and priests received from the apostles the power of changing bread and wine into the body and blood of Christ.

280. When do the bishops and priests change bread and wine into the body and blood of Christ?

The bishops and priests change bread and wine into the body and blood of Christ in the Mass.

281. After the consecration, what is on the altar in the place of bread and wine?

After the consecration there is on the altar in the place of bread and wine, the body and blood of Jesus Christ.

282. What remains of the bread and wine after the consecration?

Only the appearances of bread and wine remain after the consecration.

283. What is meant by appearances of bread and wine?

By appearances of bread and wine is meant all that the senses perceive of bread and wine: the color, taste, etc.

284. Under how many appearances is Jesus present?

Jesus is present under two appearances: those of bread and wine.

285. Is Jesus present whole and entire under each appearance?

Jesus is present whole and entire under each appearance.

286. Is Jesus present whole and entire in each particle of the appearances of bread and wine?

Jesus is present whole and entire in each particle of the appearances of bread and wine.

287. How long does Jesus remain present in the Blessed Sacrament?

Jesus remains present in the Blessed Sacrament as long as the appearances exist.

288. What must we do because Jesus is present in the Blessed Sacrament?

Because Jesus is present in the Blessed Sacrament, we must adore the Blessed Sacrament.

Genuflection. Holy hour. Forty Hours' Devotion.

289. Why did Jesus institute the Blessed Sacrament?

Jesus instituted the Blessed Sacrament
  1. to honor the Blessed Trinity (Mass);
  2. to be the food of our souls (Holy Communion).

Application. When we pass a church we should greet our Savior with a short prayer. (Praised be Jesus Christ. O Sacrament most holy, O Sacrament divine, all praise and all thanksgiving, be every moment Thine.) Let us frequently visit our Lord in the Blessed Sacrament and love to attend the Benediction service. It is a privilege to contribute to the ornamentation of altar, tabernacle, and sanctuary. This will please Jesus and bring us a rich reward.

2. THE HOLY SACRIFICE OF THE MASS

290. What is a sacrifice?

A sacrifice is a visible gift offered to God.

291. Why is sacrifice offered?

Sacrifice is offered to adore, thank, implore, and propitiate God.

292. What is required for a sacrifice?

For a sacrifice is required
1. a visible gift (victim, host)
2. a priest
3. an altar.

293. Which is the perfect sacrifice?

The perfect sacrifice is the sacrifice of Jesus on the cross.

"By one oblation He hath perfected forever them that are sanctified" (Heb. 10:14).

294. Is the sacrifice of the cross still offered?

The sacrifice of the cross is still offered in every Mass.

"From the rising of the sun even to the going down, My name is great among the Gentiles, and in every place there is a sacrifice, and there is offered to My name a clean oblation" (Mal. 1:11).

295. How does Jesus offer Himself in the Mass?

Jesus offers Himself in the Mass to the Blessed Trinity in an unbloody manner.

296. When did Jesus institute the holy sacrifice of the Mass?

Jesus instituted the holy sacrifice of the Mass at the Last Supper.

"Do this for a commemoration of Me" (Luke 22:19).

297. Who is the invisible priest in the Mass?

The invisible priest in the Mass is Jesus Christ.

298. How is the Mass divided?

The Mass is divided into
1. the preparatory and instructive part (Mass of the catechumens);
2. the sacrificial part (Mass of the faithful).

See page 110.

299. Which are the principal parts of the Mass?

The principal parts of the Mass are:
1. the offertory
2. the consecration
3. the communion.

300. Who are specially benefited by the Mass?

Those specially benefited by the Mass are:
1. the priest who celebrates the Mass
2. those for whom it is especially offered
3. all who take part in it.

301. Why is the Mass offered?

The Mass is offered

1. to honor the Blessed Trinity;
2. to distribute the graces which Christ earned by His death on the cross.

Definition: The Mass is the perfect sacrifice of the New Testament in which Jesus Christ offers Himself to the Blessed Trinity under the appearances of bread and wine.

The Mass is a sacrifice of adoration, thanksgiving, expiation, and petition.

Application. The holiest action that takes place on earth is the Mass. We should go to Mass often, be attentive during the instructive part, and devout during the sacrificial part. The best way to take part in the Mass is to unite with the priest in prayer by using a missal and to receive the Holy Eucharist. It is an honor to serve the priest at Mass.

3. HOLY COMMUNION

The act of receiving the Holy Eucharist is called Holy Communion.

302. What are the effects of Holy Communion?

The effects of Holy Communion are:

1. it unites us most intimately with Christ;
2. it increases sanctifying grace in us;
3. it weakens our evil inclinations;
4. it strengthens us in the practice of all virtues;
5. it cleanses us from venial sins;
6. it preserves us from mortal sins;
7. it is a pledge of eternal life.

Pledge=guarantee.

"He that eateth My flesh, and drinketh My blood, abideth in Me and I in Him" (John 6:57). "He that eateth My flesh and drinketh My blood hath everlasting life and I will raise him up in the last day" (John 6:55).

303. How must we receive the Holy Eucharist to obtain the graces of this sacrament?

To obtain the graces of this sacrament we must receive the Holy Eucharist worthily.

304. Who receives the Holy Eucharist worthily?

He receives the Holy Eucharist worthily who receives it in the state of sanctifying grace.

Venial sins do not render Holy Communion unworthy, but they lessen the effects.

305. Who receives the Holy Eucharist unworthily?

He receives the Holy Eucharist unworthily who knowingly receives it in the state of mortal sin.

306. Why is an unworthy Communion a fearful crime?

An unworthy Communion is a fearful crime because it is a horrible sacrilege.

"Whosoever shall eat this bread or drink the chalice of the Lord unworthily, shall be guilty of the body and of the blood of the Lord." "For he that eateth and drinketh unworthily, eateth and drinketh judgment to himself, not discerning the body of the Lord" (I Cor. 11:27, 29).

307. How often should we receive the Holy Eucharist?

We should receive the Holy Eucharist frequently.

The Church recommends daily Communion.

For daily Communion there are two requisites:
1. to be free from mortal sin;
2. to have a right intention.

308. How must we prepare for Holy Communion?

To prepare for Holy Communion we must:
1. make a good confession to cleanse ourselves from mortal sin;
2. fast, that is, take no food or alcoholic drinks for one hour or other liquids for one hour, except water, which may be taken at any time.*

"Let a man prove himself, and so let him eat of that bread, and drink of the chalice" (I Cor. 11:28).

309. How should we approach and leave the holy table?

We should approach and leave the holy table with the greatest reverence.

Instructions for receiving the Holy Eucharist. Walk to the communion rail with your hands folded and your eyes cast down. At the rail hold the paten so as to prevent the sacred host from falling to the floor by accident. Hold your head erect, extend the tongue a little over the lower lip. Go back to your place reverently. Spend ten or fifteen minutes in devout prayer. Outside of the Mass use the Communion prayers in your prayerbook.

Application. Let us have a great desire of Holy Communion and receive the Holy Eucharist frequently. We can never be happier or richer than when we receive God into our heart. He is the author and source of all graces.

PENANCE

310. What happens in the sacrament of penance?

In the sacrament of penance the priest forgives sins.

Definition: Penance is the sacrament in which the priest by judicial sentence remits sins committed after baptism to those who confess them contritely.

*This question has been changed in this printing to reflect the current rules.

311. From whom did the priest receive the power to forgive sins?

The priest received the power to forgive sins from God; in the sacrament of holy orders.

Jesus breathed on the apostles and said to them: " Receive ye the Holy Ghost. Whose sins you shall forgive, they are forgiven them; and whose sins you shall retain, they are retained" (John 20:22, 23).

312. Who must receive the sacrament of penance?

Everyone who has committed a mortal sin after baptism must receive the sacrament of penance.

313. What does the sacrament of penance take away?

The sacrament of penance takes away
1. all mortal sins,
2. all venial sins for which we are sorry and which we confess,
3. the eternal punishment,
4. at least a part of the temporal punishment.

314. What does the sacrament of penance give us?

The sacrament of penance gives us
1. sanctifying grace if it was lost;
2. an increase of sanctifying grace, if it was not lost;
3. many special graces for a devout life (actual graces).

315. What must we do to receive the sacrament of penance worthily?

To receive the sacrament of penance worthily we must
1. invoke the Holy Ghost,

2. examine our conscience,
3. be sorry for our sins,
4. make a firm purpose of amendment,
5. confess our sins,
6. have the intention of making satisfaction.

Three essentials: contrition, confession, satisfaction,

1. We Should Invoke the Holy Ghost

316. Why should we invoke the Holy Ghost?

We should invoke the Holy Ghost that He may help us to make a good confession.

"Come, O Holy Ghost, and help me, that I may know my sins, be heartily sorry for them, and confess them sincerely."

2. We Must Examine Our Conscience

317. How do we examine our conscience?

We examine our conscience by calling to mind how we have failed against the commandments of God and the Church and the duties of our state of life.

See the table of sins on page 100.

3. We Must Be Sorry for Our Sins

318. Which is the most necessary part of our preparation for confession?

The most necessary part of our preparation for confession is contrition.

319. Why must we be sorry for our sins?

We must be sorry for our sins because we have offended God by them.

Contrition=sorrow for sin.

Contrition must be sincere, not in words only.

Contrition must be universal, including all mortal sins.

Contrition must be supernatural; we must be sorry for our sins on account of God. Natural sorrow (on account of disgrace, scolding, temporal loss) is of no value in the sacrament of penance. Supernatural sorrow is of two kinds: *imperfect,* which arises mostly from fear of God's justice; and *perfect,* which arises from the love of God. Perfect contrition takes away sin even before confession.

We should make an act of perfect contrition:

1. when we have committed a mortal sin,
2. whenever we are in danger,
3. as a part of our evening prayer,
4. at confession,
5. before Holy Communion, for our venial sins.

Perfect contrition does not excuse us from confession and it does not entitle us to receive Holy Communion.

320. For what sins must we be sorry?

We must be sorry at least for all our mortal sins.

If we have been guilty of venial sins only, we must be sorry for at least one of them; or we may include in our contrition and confession sins of our past life for which we are especially sorry.

4. We Must Make a Firm Purpose of Amendment

321. Who has a firm purpose of amendment?

He has a firm purpose of amendment who is determined to do better and never again commit a mortal sin.

See the act of contrition (which includes the firm purpose of amendment) on page 97; also the one in your prayerbook.

5. We Must Confess Our Sins

322. Why must we confess our sins?

We must confess our sins because Jesus Christ commanded it when He said to His apostles: "Whose sins you shall forgive, they are forgiven them; and whose sins you shall retain, they are retained."

Confess=to tell.

323. What sins must we confess?

We must confess all our mortal sins.

324. How must we confess our sins?

We must confess our sins according to kind and number.

325. Is it necessary to confess venial sins?

It is not necessary to confess venial sins, but it is good and advisable to do so.

326. Who receives the sacrament of penance unworthily?

He receives the sacrament of penance unworthily
1. who is not sorry for his sins;
2. who does not tell all the mortal sins that he remembers;
3. who does not intend to make satisfaction.

In an unworthy confession no sins are forgiven.

Whoever forgets some sins makes a good confession. His sins are forgiven, but he must mention the forgotten sins in his next confession.

The penitent kneels and begins his confession thus: "Bless me, Father, for I have sinned. My last confession was ... ago. I have committed the following sins:"

He concludes by saying: "That is all, Father." (Or: "I include from my past life the sins against the ... commandment. That is all, Father.")

327. Is the priest ever allowed to tell anything he has heard in confession?

The priest is never allowed to tell anything he has heard in confession.

Seal of confession. Example: St. John Nepomucene, died 1393.

General confession=one in which we repeat all or several confessions of our past life. It is necessary if one or more confessions have been bad. It is advisable on special occasions.

6. We Must Make Satisfaction

328. What is meant by making satisfaction?

By making satisfaction is meant performing the penance given by the priest in confession.

329. Why does the priest give us a penance in confession?

The priest gives us a penance in confession in order

1. that we may expiate the temporal punishment,
2. that we may amend our life.

330. How does the priest give absolution?

The priest gives absolution by saying: "I absolve thee from thy sins in the name of the Father, and of the Son, and of the Holy Ghost. Amen."

Application. Everyone should go to confession often. We should prepare well and should be humble and sincere at confession. It is better not to go to confession at all than to make a bad confession. When we have had the misfortune to commit mortal sin, we should not postpone confession. We might die suddenly and be eternally lost.

Indulgences

331. How is temporal punishment remitted?

Temporal punishment is remitted by performance of the penance imposed, by fasting, other good works, pious use of sacramentals, indulgences, and purgatory.

Definition: An indulgence is the remission of the temporal punishment due to sin.

332. Who can grant indulgences?

The pope, as Vicar of Jesus Christ, can grant indulgences.

"Whatsoever thou shalt loose on earth, it shall be loosed also in heaven" (Matt. 16:19).

333. What must we do to gain an indulgence?

To gain an indulgence we must
  1. be in the state of grace,
  2. exactly perform the good works prescribed.

Plenary indulgence, remission of all temporal punishment.

Partial indulgence, remission of a part of the temporal punishment.

See your prayerbook about prayers to which an indulgence is attached.

Application. It is a good Catholic practice to recite the ejaculatory prayers to which an indulgence has been attached.

EXTREME UNCTION

334. Who ought to receive extreme unction?

Everyone who has come to the use of reason and who is dangerously sick ought to receive extreme unction.

Extreme=last; unction=anointing.

335. How does the priest administer extreme unction?

The priest administers extreme unction by anointing the eyes, ears, nose, lips, hands, and feet of the sick person, and saying: "Through this holy unction, and of His tender mercy, may the Lord pardon thee whatsoever sins thou hast committed by thy sight, hearing, etc."

336. What benefits does extreme unction confer on the soul?

Extreme unction confers these benefits on the soul:
1. it increases sanctifying grace,
2. it remits venial sins and those mortal sins which the sick person cannot confess,
3. it gives strength in suffering and temptations.

"Is any man sick among you? Let him bring in the priests of the Church, and let them pray over him, anointing him with oil in the name of the Lord. And the prayer of faith shall save the sick man, and the Lord shall raise him up, and if he be in sins, they shall be forgiven him" (Jas. 5:14, 15).

337. Does extreme unction sometimes restore a person's health?

Extreme unction sometimes does restore a person's health, if such is God's holy will.

338. When should a sick person receive extreme unction?

A sick person should receive extreme unction while he is still conscious.

339. What should be prepared in the sickroom for the administration of the last sacraments?

For the administration of the last sacraments there should be prepared in the sick room:

1. a table covered with a white cloth,
2. on the table a crucifix,
3. on each side of the crucifix a blessed candle,
4. holy water with sprinkler,
5. cotton or bread (for removing oil),
6. a glass of water with a spoon.

Procedure in the sickroom:
1. sprinkling with holy water
2. confession
3. Holy Communion
4. Extreme unction
5. plenary indulgence.

Application. When a person is seriously sick he ought to send for the priest in time, so that he may be able to receive the last sacraments while he is fully conscious. Let us pray often, while in health, that we may have the grace of a happy death, and that we may not depart this life without the sacraments.

HOLY ORDERS

340. Who administers the sacrament of holy orders?

The bishop administers the sacrament of holy orders.

341. How does the bishop administer the holy order of priesthood?

The bishop administers the holy order of priesthood by imposing hands upon those to be ordained, invoking the Holy Ghost upon them, anointing their hands, delivering to them the sacred vessels with bread and wine, and clothing them with the sacred vestments.

"And they praying, imposed hands upon them" (Acts 6:6).

342. What power does the priest chiefly receive in ordination?

In ordination the priest chiefly receives the power to celebrate Mass and to forgive sins.

343. What special grace does the priest receive in ordination?

In ordination the priest receives the special grace to discharge his duties well.

"I admonish thee that thou stir up the grace of God which is in thee by the imposition of my hands" (II Tim. 1:6).

The three highest degrees of the sacrament of holy orders are: deaconship, priesthood, and episcopate (=order of bishop).

A ceremony (tonsure), four minor orders (those of doorkeeper, reader, exorcist and acolyte), and two major orders (those of subdeacon and deacon), precede ordination to the priesthood.

Application. Priests are God's representatives; we should respect them. They are our greatest spiritual benefactors; therefore we should be grateful to them. They take care of our eternal welfare; therefore we should contribute to their support. "They that serve the altar, partake with the altar." Let us often pray for our priests, as they do for us.

MATRIMONY

344. Why is matrimony holy?

Matrimony is holy:
1. because God Himself instituted it;
2. because Christ made it a sacrament.

"This is a great sacrament" (Ephes. 5:32).

Definition: Marriage is a sacrament in which a man and a woman give themselves to each other for life.

345. What should be the chief concern of a person who intends to marry?

The chief concern of a person who intends to marry should be to select a good Catholic as husband or wife.

"House and riches are given by parents; but a prudent wife is properly from the Lord" (Prov. 19:14).

346. How do groom and bride receive the sacrament of matrimony?

Groom and bride receive the sacrament of matrimony by declaring in the presence of the pastor and two witnesses that they take each other for husband and wife.

Nuptial Mass. Blessing of the ring. Bridal blessing.

347. Can the bond of marriage ever be dissolved?

The bond of marriage can never be dissolved except by death.

"What therefore God hath joined together, let no man put asunder" (Matt. 19:6).

While husband and wife are living, neither of them can remarry.

348. What grace does the sacrament of matrimony give?

The sacrament of matrimony gives to the married couple the grace to fulfill the duties of their state.

349. Which are the most important duties of married people towards each other?

The most important duties of married people towards each other are to live in mutual love and fidelity.

350. Which is the chief duty of parents to their children?

The chief duty of parents to their children is to give them a good Christian education.

Application. Matrimony is a holy state. It is also a difficult and responsible state. Without the blessing of God no one can be happy in this state, therefore it should be entered with God's blessing, according to the rules and wishes of His Holy Church. Whoever enters this state in mortal sin, commits a sacrilege.

PRAYER

351. What do we mean by "prayer"?

By "prayer" we mean the raising of our soul to God to speak to Him.

Mental prayer=prayer with the mind only.

Vocal prayer=prayer expressed in words.

"Lip" prayer=reciting the words but thinking about other things.

To meditate=to ponder over religious truths and to apply them to oneself by a practical resolution.

352. Why do we pray?

We pray
1. to praise God
2. to thank Him
3. to beseech Him.

353. Why must we pray?

We must pray
1. because God has commanded it;
2. because without prayer we cannot remain in the grace of God.

"Watch ye, and pray that ye enter not into temptation" (Matt. 26:41).

354. How must we pray?

We must pray
1. with devotion
2. with confidence
3. with perseverance.

Also with humility and resignation to God's will.

355. Who prays with devotion?

He prays with devotion, who thinks of God and of what he wishes to say to God.

"This people ... with their lips glorify Me, but their heart is far from Me" (Is. 29:13).

356. Who prays with confidence?

He prays with confidence who thinks: "God will surely hear my prayer because He has promised to do so."

"All things whatsoever you ask when ye pray, believe that you shall receive, and they shall come unto you" (Mark 11:24).

357. Who prays with perseverance?

He prays with perseverance who does not cease praying although he may not be answered immediately.

"We ought always to pray and not to faint" (Luke 18:1).

Examples: The woman of Canaan (Matt. 15:22-28). St. Monica.

Parable: The importunate friend (Luke 11:5-9).

358. What may we ask of God?

We may ask of God everything that is necessary or useful for body and soul.

359. What should we especially ask of God?

We should especially ask of God that we may gain heaven.

360. Why do we not always obtain what we ask for?

We do not always obtain what we ask for

1. because we do not always pray as we ought;
2. because what we ask for is not always good for us.

"You know not what you ask" (Matt. 20:22).

361. For whom should we pray?

We should pray for ourselves and for others, especially for our parents and relatives, for friends and enemies, and for the souls in purgatory.

362. Where can we pray?

We can pray everywhere, because God is everywhere.

363. Where especially can we pray well?

We can pray well especially in church.

"My eyes shall be open, and My ears attentive to the prayer of him that shall pray in this place" (II Par. 7:15).

364. When can we pray?

We can pray at all times.

365. When, in particular, should we pray?

We should pray in particular

1. every morning and evening;
2. before and after meals;
3. on Sundays and holydays;
4. in every necessity and temptation.

Family prayer: "Where there are two or three gathered together in My name, there am I in the midst of them" (Matt. 18:20).

Application. We should love and practice prayer. It is a great honor that we are permitted to speak to God. It is so easy to pray: we can do so at all times in all places. A child loves to speak to his father; a child of God loves to speak to God. By prayer we honor God and may obtain everything. "He that knows how to pray well, knows also how to live well" (St. Augustine). He that lives well, will also die well.

THE LORD'S PRAYER

Our Father, who art in heaven;
  hallowed be Thy name;
  Thy kingdom come;
  Thy will be done on earth as it is in heaven.
  Give us this day our daily bread;
  and forgive us our trespasses, as we forgive those
    who trespass against us;
  and lead us not into temptation;
  but deliver us from evil. Amen.

366. Why is the Our Father the best of all prayers?

The Our Father is the best of all prayers because Christ Himself taught it.

(Matt. 6:9-13; Luke 11:2-4.)

367. Of what parts does the Lord's Prayer consist?

The Lord's Prayer consists of an address and seven petitions.

368. For what do we pray in the first petition?

In the first petition we pray for the grace to honor and glorify God at all times.

369. For what do we pray in the second petition?

In the second petition we pray

1. that all men may come into the Church;
2. that grace may abound in our souls;
3. that all men may get to heaven.

The kingdom of God is threefold: around us (the Church); within us (grace); above us (heaven).

370. For what do we pray in the third petition?

In the third petition we pray that we may at all times do the will of God as faithfully as the angels do it in heaven.

371. For what do we pray in the fourth petition?

In the fourth petition we pray that God may give us whatever is necessary for body and soul.

372. For what do we pray in the fifth petition?

In the fifth petition we pray that God may forgive us our sins and the punishment due to them.

373. For what do we pray in the sixth petition?

In the sixth petition we pray that God may preserve us from temptations or at least give us the grace to resist them.

374. For what do we pray in the seventh petition?

In the seventh petition we pray that God may preserve us from sin and all other evils.

375. What does the word "Amen" mean?

The word "Amen" means, "So be it."

Application. Say the Our Father frequently and devoutly. Remember, it came from the most Sacred Heart of Jesus and touches the heart of the heavenly Father. It always finds a ready hearing. If you are in trouble or in need and know not how to speak to God, say the Our Father. It includes everything.

THE HAIL MARY

Hail Mary, full of grace;
the Lord is with thee;
blessed art thou among women,
and blessed is the fruit of thy womb, Jesus.
Holy Mary, Mother of God,
pray for us sinners, now and at the hour of our
death. Amen.

Angelic salutation.

376. Who composed the Hail Mary?

The archangel Gabriel, Elizabeth, and the Church composed the Hail Mary.

THE ANGELUS

377. Why is the Angelus bell rung every day?

The Angelus bell is rung every day to remind us of the incarnation of our Lord.

See page 98.

THE ROSARY

378. Why is the rosary such an excellent prayer?

The rosary is such an excellent prayer because a meditation on the chief mysteries in the lives of Jesus and Mary is added to the best vocal prayers.

Definition: A rosary=a chain with beads on which to count prayers; or, a form of prayer composed of Our Fathers and Hail Marys arranged in fifteen decades in which fifteen mysteries of our redemption are devoutly considered.

379. Which are the usual fifteen mysteries of the rosary?

The usual fifteen mysteries of the rosary are:

The five joyful mysteries:
1. The Annunciation
2. The Visitation
3. The Nativity
4. The Presentation in the Temple
5. The Finding of the Child Jesus in the Temple.

(Recited on Sundays from Advent to Lent, and on Mondays and Thursdays during the year.)

The five sorrowful mysteries:
1. The Agony in the Garden
2. The Scourging at the Pillar
3. The Crowning with Thorns
4. Jesus Carrying His Cross
5. The Crucifixion.

(Recited on Sundays in Lent, and on Tuesdays and Fridays during the year.)

The five glorious mysteries:
1. The Resurrection
2. The Ascension
3. The Descent of the Holy Ghost upon the Apostles
4. The Assumption of the Blessed Virgin Mary
5. The Crowning of the Blessed Virgin Mary.

(Recited on Sundays from Easter to Advent, and on Wednesdays and Saturdays during the year.)

Dominican rosary. Rosary month=October. Confraternity of the Rosary. Decade=one Our Father and ten Hail Marys. A plenary indulgence is granted for reciting five decades in the presence of the Blessed Sacrament.

THE STATIONS OF THE CROSS

380. Which are the fourteen stations of the cross?

The fourteen stations of the cross are:

1. Jesus is condemned to death
2. Jesus takes His cross
3. Jesus falls the first time
4. Jesus meets His afflicted Mother
5. Simon of Cyrene carries the cross of Jesus
6. Veronica presents a towel to Jesus
7. Jesus falls the second time
8. Jesus consoles the weeping women
9. Jesus falls the third time
10. Jesus is stripped of His garments
11. Jesus is nailed to the cross
12. Jesus dies on the cross
13. Jesus is taken down from the cross
14. Jesus is laid in the grave.

381. What must we do when saying the stations privately?

When saying the stations privately we must go from one station to another and meditate at each station on the sufferings of Christ.

LITANIES

382. What are litanies?

Litanies are prayers composed of many short invocations of God and the saints.

383. Which are the approved litanies?

The approved litanies are:
1. the litany of the Saints
2. the litany of the Holy Name of Jesus
3. the litany of the Sacred Heart
4. the litany of the Blessed Virgin
5. the litany of St. Joseph.

THE SIGN OF THE CROSS

In the name of the Father, and of the Son, and of
the Holy Ghost. Amen.

384. How does a Catholic profess his faith?

A Catholic professes his faith by making the sign
of the cross.

385. When is the sign of the cross particularly efficacious?

The sign of the cross is particularly efficacious when
the Church uses it in blessings and consecrations.

386. Why are persons, places, and things blessed?

Persons, places, and things are blessed to call God's
protection upon them or upon those who use them.

The sick, children, brides, mothers; houses, schools, bridges,
hospitals; water, candles, palms, ashes, crucifixes.

A sacramental is a thing blessed by the Church, the pious
use of which obtains spiritual benefits for us. The sign of the
cross also is a sacramental.

387. Why are persons, places, and things consecrated?

Persons, places, and things are consecrated to set
them aside for divine service.

Churches, chalices, altar-stones, holy oils.

388. Why do we use blessed articles?

We use blessed articles

1. because they protect us against the devil and many evils;

2. because they obtain for us blessings for soul and body.

Application. The Church blesses many things. Have your home and your automobile blessed. Keep some blessed candles on hand. Holy water should be found in every home. Take holy water as you enter the church. It refreshes your soul as rain refreshes plants.

PRAYERS

In the name of the Father, and of the Son, and of the Holy Ghost. Amen.

THE LORD'S PRAYER

Our Father, who art in heaven; hallowed be Thy name; Thy kingdom come; Thy will be done on earth as it is in heaven. Give us this day our daily bread; and forgive us our trespasses, as we forgive those who trespass against us; and lead us not into temptation; but deliver us from evil. Amen.

THE ANGELIC SALUTATION

Hail Mary, full of grace, the Lord is with thee; blessed art thou among women, and blessed is the fruit of thy womb, Jesus. Holy Mary, Mother of God, pray for us sinners, now and at the hour of our death. Amen.

THE APOSTLES' CREED

I believe in God, the Father Almighty, Creator of heaven and earth; and in Jesus Christ, His only Son, our Lord, who was conceived by the Holy Ghost, born of the Virgin Mary; suffered under Pontius Pilate, was crucified; died, and was buried; He descended into hell; the third day He arose again from the dead; He ascended into heaven, sitteth at the right hand of God, the Father Almighty; from thence He shall come to judge the living and the dead. I believe in the Holy Ghost; the Holy Catholic Church; the communion of saints; the forgiveness of sins, the resurrection of the body, and life everlasting. Amen.

THE DOXOLOGY

Glory be to the Father, and to the Son, and to the Holy Ghost. As it was in the beginning, is now, and ever shall be, world without end. Amen.

AN ACT OF FAITH

O my God, I firmly believe that Thou art one God in three Divine Persons, Father, Son, and Holy Ghost; I believe that Thy Divine Son became man, and died for our sins, and that He will come to judge the living and the dead. I believe these and all truths which the Holy Catholic Church teaches, because Thou hast revealed them, who canst neither deceive nor be deceived.

AN ACT OF HOPE

O my God, relying on Thy almighty power and infinite mercy and promises, I hope to obtain pardon of my sins, the help of Thy grace, and life everlasting, through the merits of Jesus Christ, my Lord and Redeemer.

AN ACT OF CHARITY

O my God, I love Thee above all things, with my whole heart and soul, because Thou art all-good and worthy of all love. I love my neighbor as myself for the love of Thee. I forgive all who have injured me, and ask pardon of all whom I have injured.

AN ACT OF CONTRITION

O my God, I am heartily sorry for having offended Thee, and I detest all my sins, because of Thy just punishments, but most of all because they offend Thee, my God, who art all-good and deserving of all my love. I firmly resolve, with the help of Thy grace, to sin no more and to avoid the near occasions of sin.

Or: O my God, I am heartily sorry for having offended Thee, because Thou art all-good; and I firmly purpose by the help of Thy grace not to offend Thee again.

TO THE GUARDIAN ANGEL

Angel of God, my guardian dear,
To whom His love commits me here,
Ever this day (night) be at my side,
To light and guard, to rule and guide. Amen.

BEFORE MEALS

Bless us, O Lord, and these thy gifts, which we are about to receive from Thy bounty, through Christ our Lord. Amen.

AFTER MEALS

We give Thee thanks for all Thy benefits, O Almighty God, who livest and reignest forever; and may the souls of the faithful departed, through the mercy of God, rest in peace. Amen.

THE ANGELUS

The Angel of the Lord declared unto Mary.
And she conceived of the Holy Ghost.

   Hail Mary, etc.

Behold the handmaid of the Lord.
Be it done unto me according to thy word.

   Hail Mary, etc.

And the Word was made flesh.
And dwelt among us.

   Hail Mary, etc.

Pray for us, O Holy Mother of God,
That we may be made worthy of the promises of
   Christ.

Let us pray

Pour forth, we beseech Thee, O Lord, Thy grace into
our hearts; that as we have known the incarnation of
Christ Thy Son by the message of an angel, so, by
His passion and cross, we may be brought to the glory
of His resurrection; through the same Christ our Lord.
Amen.

DURING EASTER TIME

O Queen of heaven, rejoice! Alleluia.
For He whom thou didst merit to bear, Alleluia.
Hath arisen, as He said, Alleluia.
Pray for us to God, Alleluia.
Rejoice and be glad, O Virgin Mary, Alleluia.
For the Lord hath risen indeed.   Alleluia.

Let us pray

O God, who through the resurrection of Thy Son our Lord, Jesus Christ, didst vouchsafe to fill the world with joy; grant, we beseech Thee, that, through His Virgin Mother, Mary, we may lay hold on the joys of everlasting life. Through the same Christ our Lord. Amen.

SALVE REGINA

Hail holy Queen, Mother of mercy; our life, our sweetness and our hope. To thee do we cry, poor banished children of Eve; to thee do we send up our sighs, mourning and weeping in this valley of tears. Turn, then, most gracious advocate, thine eyes of mercy towards us, and after this our exile, show unto us the blessed fruit of thy womb Jesus; O clement, O loving, O sweet Virgin Mary.

NIGHT PRAYER

I lay my body down to sleep,
I pray to God my soul to keep.
And if I die before I wake,
I ask of God my soul to take.

THE ROSARY

See page 91.

CONFESSION

1. "Come, Holy Ghost, and help me, that I may know my sins, be heartily sorry for them, and confess them sincerely."

2. Examination of conscience. The following is not a complete list of all sins.

Some sins against the first commandment: habitually to neglect morning, evening, and meal prayers; to pray with wilful distraction; to receive a sacrament unworthily; to be ashamed of one's religion.

Some sins against the second commandment: to use God's name irreverently, to curse; to swear a false oath.

Some sins against the third commandment: to miss Mass on Sunday or a holyday through one's fault; to come late to Mass; to do forbidden work on Sunday; to misbehave in the church.

Some sins against the fourth commandment: to disobey parents (or other superiors); to talk back to them; to grieve them; to make them angry; to wish them evil; to speak ill of them; to resist their corrections; not to assist them in old age; to make fun of old people.

Some sins against the fifth commandment: to hurt others, to quarrel, to hate others, to be angry at them; to wish others evil; to lead others into sin.

Some sins against the sixth and ninth commandments: to think of impure things, desire them, speak of them; to listen to impure talk with pleasure; to gaze at impure things or pictures; to read filthy magazines; to commit impurity alone or with others.

Some sins against the seventh and tenth commandments: to steal, to cheat, to damage the property of others; to keep valuable things that were found; to accept stolen goods; to wish to steal.

Some sins against the eighth commandment: to tell lies; to tell the hidden faults of others, to slander others; to have false suspicion.

Some sins against the precepts of the Church: to eat meat on days of abstinence.*

Some sins against the duties of one's state of life: to neglect to study; to cheat in school; to be proud; to be lazy.

3. Contrition and firm purpose of amendment. Consider the punishment of hell and purgatory; the sufferings and death of Jesus Christ; the goodness of God. Recite an act of contrition.

O my God, I am heartily sorry for having offended Thee, because Thou art all-good; and I firmly purpose by the help of Thy grace not to offend Thee again.

O my God! I am heartily sorry for all my sins because by them I have offended Thee who art so good. I am firmly resolved to amend my life and to sin no more. Dear Jesus, who died upon the cross for me, forgive me all my sins.

4. Confession. Enter the confessional, kneel, and say: "Bless me, Father, for I have sinned. My last confession was ... ago. I did these sins ... .

Finish by saying: "That is all, Father." Or: "I include the sins against the ... commandment from my past life. That is all, Father."

Repeat a short act of contrition while the priest is giving you absolution. Leave the confessional when he says: "Go in peace."

5. Satisfaction. If you have time, say your penance before you leave the church, and thank God for the grace of the sacrament.

*This question has been changed in this printing to reflect the current rules.

BOOKS OF THE BIBLE

OLD TESTAMENT

21 Historical Books

5 Books of Moses
Josue
Judges
Ruth
4 Books of Kings
2 Books of Chronicles
Esdras
Nehemias
Tobias
Judith
Esther
2 Books of the Macha-
bees

7 Moral Books

Job
The Psalms
Proverbs
Ecclesiastes
Canticle of Canticles
Wisdom
Ecclesiasticus

16 Prophetical Books

Isaias, Jeremias with Baruch,
Ezechiel, Daniel; Osee, Joel, Amos,
Abdias, Jonas, Micheas, Nahum, Habacuc,
Sophonias, Aggeus, Zacharias, Malachias.

NEW TESTAMENT

4 Gospels

St. Matthew
St. Mark
St. Luke
St. John

Acts of the Apostles
14 Epistles of St. Paul

1 to the Romans
2 to the Corinthians
1 to the Galatians
1 to the Ephesians
1 to the Philippians
1 to the Colossians
2 to the Thessalonians
2 to Timothy
1 to Titus
1 to Philemon
1 to the Hebrews

1 Epistle of St. Jude
1 Epistle of St. James
2 Epistles of St. Peter
3 Epistles of St. John
The Apocalypse of St. John.

PART IV

LITURGY

Liturgy is the official worship by the Church. It consists in the Mass, the administration of the sacraments, the recitation of the divine office, and the blessings of the Church.

Popular devotions are: the rosary, the way of the cross, benediction of the Blessed Sacrament, novenas.

Liturgical books are: the missal, the breviary, the ritual.

Rite is the form, prescribed by the Church, in which the prayers and ceremonies are to be carried out.

Ceremonies are the motions which accompany prayer. For example, genuflection, bowing, folding of hands.

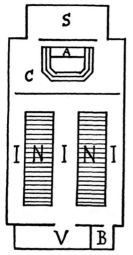

PARTS OF A CHURCH

C=choir or sanctuary
A=altar
S =sacristy
N=nave
I =aisle
V=vestibule
B=baptistery
    gallery
    campanile or bell-tower
    chapel.

FURNITURE IN A CHURCH

Altar, pulpit, communion rail, credence, holy water fonts, baptismal font, organ, confessional, ambry, pews, sanctuary lamp.

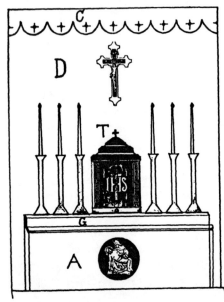

THE ALTAR

A. altar table (a wooden altar has an altar-stone)

T. tabernacle

D. dossal=curtain back of the altar

G. gradine or candle-bench

C. canopy

APPURTENANCES OF THE ALTAR

Altar-stone (in a wooden altar)
Linen cloths (3)
Crucifix
Tabernacle
Missal-stand or cushion
Missal
Sanctuary lamp

Candlesticks with candles

Antependium= cloth hanging in front of the altar

Altar-stone

Missal-stand

Missal

SACRED VESSELS

Chalice

Paten

Holywater Pot

Ciborium

Monstrance

Oil Stocks

Cruets

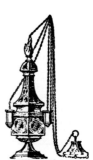

Pyx
for sick calls

Thurible

THE CHALICE PREPARED FOR MASS

Chalice
Purificator (linen cloth to wipe the
  chalice)
Paten
Host or altar bread
Pall, square piece of stiff linen to
  cover the chalice

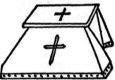

Veil of silk to
cover the chalice

Burse,
pocket containing
the corporal

Corporal, a square piece of linen laid
  on the altar-stone; the chalice and
  sacred host are placed on it.

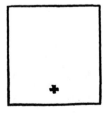

SACRED VESTMENTS

Cassock

Alb=long white
garment reaching
to the feet

Amice=
shoulder-cloth

Cincture=
girdle

Surplice

Maniple,
worn on the
left sleeve

Stole,
worn about
the neck

Biretta

SACRED VESTMENTS

Cope

Chasuble

Miter

Crozier   Dalmatic   Humeral veil

COLOR OF THE VESTMENTS

White signifies joy and glory; it is used on feasts of our Lord, of the Blessed Virgin, of the angels, and of saints that are not martyrs.

Red signifies fire and blood; it is used on Pentecost and feasts of the Holy Cross and of martyrs.

Green signifies hope; it is used on ordinary Sundays after Epiphany and Pentecost.

Violet signifies humility and penance; it is used in Advent, Lent, on Ember days and vigils.

Black signifies sorrow and mourning; it is used on Good Friday, All Souls Day; for funerals and votive Masses for the dead.

LITURGICAL TERMS

A low Mass is one in which all the prayers are merely recited.

A dialogue Mass is one in which the congregation makes the responses and joins with the priest in some of the prayers in Latin.

A conventual Mass is one which is celebrated daily in a monastery in the presence of all the monks.

A high Mass is one in which some of the parts are sung by the priest and the congregation or choir.

A solemn Mass is one which is sung by the priest assisted by deacon and subdeacon.

A pontifical Mass is a solemn Mass sung by a bishop or abbot.

Matins and lauds are those parts of the breviary or divine office which are recited or sung early in the morning, corresponding to morning prayer.

Vespers are that part of the breviary which is recited or sung in the afternoon.

Compline is that part of the breviary which is recited or sung in the evening, corresponding to night prayer.

ORDER OF THE MASS

PREPARATORY PART—I speak to God

I pray	Prayers at the foot of the altar
	Introit†
	Kyrie eleison
	Gloria*
	Collect†

INSTRUCTIVE PART—God speaks to me

I listen	Epistle† with Gradual†
	Tract*
	Sequence*
	Gospel†
	Sermon*

Nicene Creed*

THE SACRIFICE—Christ offers Himself

1. Offertory	Offertory chant†
	Offering of the bread
	Serving of the wine
I give	Offering the wine
	Washing the fingers
	Orate fratres
	Secreta†
2. Consecration	Preface
	Sanctus
I adore	Canon, memento of the living
	Consecration
	Canon, memento of the dead
3. Communion	Pater noster
	Pax Domini
	Agnus Dei
	Communion of the priest
I receive	Communion of the people
	Communion verse†
	Postcommunion prayers†
	Blessing*
	Last Gospel

Parts marked with † vary and are called the "Proper" of the Mass.

Parts marked with * do not occur in every Mass.

THE ECCLESIASTICAL YEAR

The liturgical year is the annual celebration of the mysteries of man's salvation and the memory of the saints.

The purpose of the liturgical year is to honor God and to instruct, edify, and sanctify man.

The liturgical year is made up of Sundays, feast days, octaves, fast days, and vigils.

The liturgical year is divided into three periods; two of them surround the principal feasts.

THE CHRISTMAS CYCLE

4 Sundays of Advent (violet)
  Christmas (white)
1 Sunday after Christmas (white)
  Circumcision (white)
  Epiphany (white)
6 Sundays after Epiphany (green)

THE EASTER CYCLE

Septuagesima
Sexagesima } pre-Lent (violet)
Quinquagesima

Ash Wednesday
4 Sundays
Passion Sunday } Lent (violet)
Palm Sunday
Holy Week

Easter (white)
5 Sundays after Easter (white)
  Ascension (white)

Novena (9 days) including the rogation days (3)
Sunday after Ascension (white)
Pentecost or Whitsunday (red)

THE PERIOD AFTER PENTECOST

24 Sundays after Pentecost (green)

There are 52 Sundays in the liturgical year; but 53 when New Year's Day falls on a Sunday.

Since Easter is a movable feast (the first Sunday after the full moon after the Spring equinox—between March 22 and April 25) there may be less than 6 Sundays after Epiphany. In that case the latter Sundays after Epiphany are inserted after the 23d Sunday after Pentecost. Those who use a missal should consult a Catholic calendar.

The third Sunday in Advent is called Gaudette Sunday.

The fourth Sunday in Lent is called Laetare Sunday.

The period from Passion Sunday to Holy Saturday is called Passiontide.

The week from Palm Sunday to Holy Saturday is called Holy Week.

The Sunday after Easter is also called Low Sunday.

Calendar of Feasts and Saints

	January	February	March
1	Circumcision	Ignatius, Brigid	Roger
2		Candlemas	
3	Genevieve	Blase	Cunigundis
4	Angela	Andrew Corsini	Casimir, Lucius
5		Agatha, Adelaide	
6	Epiphany	Titus, Dorothy, Gerald	Perpetua, Felicitas
7		Romuald	Thomas Aquinas
8		John of Matha	John of God
9	Julian	Cyril of Alexandria, Apollonia	Frances of Rome
10		Scholastica	Forty Martyrs
11	Hyginus	Our Lady of Lourdes	
12			Gregory I
13		Catharine Ricci	
14	Hilary	Valentine	Matilda
15	Paul (hermit)	Faustus, Jovita, Claude	Louise de Marillac
16	Marcellus	Juliana	
17	Anthony (hermit)	Faustinus	Patrick
18	St. Peter's Chair	Simeon	Christian
19	Canute		Joseph
20	Fabian, Sebastian		Cuthbert
21	Agnes		Benedict
22	Vincent, Anastasius		Renilda
23	Raymond, Emerentia	Peter Damian	
24	Timothy	Matthias	Gabriel (angel)
25	Conversion of St. Paul	Walburga	Annunciation
26	Polycarp		
27	John Chrysostom	Gabriel (Passionist)	John of Damascus
28		Roman	John Capistran
29	Francis de Sales		
30	Martina		Amadee (Gottlieb)
31	John Bosco, Marcella		

	April	May	June
1	Hugh	Philip, James	Marcellinus, Justin
2	Francis of Paula	Athanasius	
3	Richard, Irene	Finding of the Cross, Alexander	Kevin, Adolf
4	Isidore	Monica	Francis Carraciolo Walter
5	Vincent Ferrer, Juliana	Pius V	Boniface
6			Norbert
7	Herman Joseph	Stanislaus	
8			
9		Gregory Nazianzen	Primus, Felician
10		Antoninus	Margaret
11	Leo I		Barnabas
12		Achille, Pancratius	John of Facundo
13	Hermengild, Ida	Robert Bellarmine	Anthony
14	Justin	Boniface, Gemma	Basil
15		John Baptist de la Salle	Vitus, Crescentia, Germaine Cousin
16		Ubald, John of Nepomuk	
17	Anicetus	Paschal	
18		Venantius	Ephraem
19		Peter Celestine	Juliana Falconieri
20		Bernardine of Siena	Silverius
21	Anselm		Aloysius
22	Soter, Caius,	Rita	Paulinus
23	George		Ethelred (Audry)
24	Fidelis		John the Baptist
25	Mark	Gregory VII, Urban	William
26	Cletus, Marcellinus	Philip Neri, Brendan	John, Paul
27	Peter Canisius, Zita	Bede	Ladislaus
28	Paul of the Cross, Clarence, Cronan	Augustine of Canterbury	Irenaeus
29	Peter (martyr)	Mary Magdalen of Pazzi	Peter, Paul
30	Catherine of Siena	Felix, Ferdinand, Joan of Arc	Paul
31		Angela, Petronilla	

	July	August	September
1	Precious Blood	St. Peter's Chains	Giles
2	Visitation	Alphonsus	Stephen of Hungary
3	Leo II		Sabina
4	Bertha	Dominic	Rosalia
5	Anthony Zaccaria		Lawrence Justiniani
6		Transfiguration	
7	Cyril, Methodius	Cajetan, Donatus	Regina
8	Isabel		Nativity of Mary
9	Ephraem	John Vianney	Peter Claver
10	Rufina, Ulric	Lawrence	Nicholas of Tolentino
11	Pius I	Susanna	Protus, Hyacinth
12	John of Malta	Clara	Name of Mary
13	Anacletus, Eugene	Hyppolitus	
14	Bonaventure		Exaltation of Cross
15	Henry	Assumption	7 Sorrows of Mary
16	Our Lady of Carmel	Joachim, Roch	Cornelius, Cyprian
17	Alexis	Hyacinth	Hildegard
18	Camillus, Frederick	Helen	Joseph Cupertino
19	Vincent de Paul	John Eudes	Januarius
20	Jerome Emiliani	Bernard	Eustace
21	Praxedis	Jane Frances	Matthew
22	Mary Magdalen		Thomas Villanova, Maurice
23	Liborius, Apollinaris	Philip Benizi	Linus, Thecla
24	Christina, Francis Solanus	Bartholomew	Our Lady of Ransom, Gerhard
25	James, Christopher	Louis IX	
26	Anna	Zephyrine	Isaac Jogues, Noel
27	Pantaleon, Aurelius	Joseph Calasanza	Cosmas, Damian
28	Victor	Augustine of Hippo	Wenceslaus, Lioba
29	Martha, Beatrice		Michael
30	Julitta	Rose of Lima	Jerome
31	Ignatius Loyola	Raymond	

	October	November	December
1	Remigius	All Saints	Eligius
2	Guardian Angels	All Souls	Bibiana
3	Theresa of Lisieux	Hubert, Malachy	Francis Xavier
4	Francis of Assisi	Charles Borromeo	Barbara
5	Placid	Emeric	Sabbas
6	Bruno	Leonard	Nicholas
7	Holy Rosary, Justina		Ambrose
8	Bridget of Sweden		Immaculate Conception
9	Denis	Theodore	Leocadia
10	Francis Borgia	Andrew Avellinus	
11	Maternity of Mary	Martin	Damasus
12	Wilfred, Serafin	Martin I	
13	Edmund, Theophile	Stanislaus, Didacus (Diego)	Lucy
14	Callistus	Josaphat	Berthold
15	Theresa of Avila	Gertrude, Albert	
16	Gerard Majella, Hedwig		Eusebius, Adelaide
17	Magaret Mary	Gregory Thaumaturgus	
18	Luke	Roman	
19	Peter Alcantara	Elizabeth of Hungary	
20	John Canty	Felix of Valois, Edmund	Leonard of Port Maurice
21	Hilarion, Ursula	Presentation of Mary	Thomas
22		Cecilia	Zeno
23		Clement I	
24	Raphael	John of the Cross	
25		Catharine of Alexandria	Christmas, Anastasia
26	Evaristus	Sylvester, Konrad	Stephen
27			John
28	Simon, Jude, Eunice		Holy Innocents
29		Salvatore	Thomas of Canterbury
30	Alphonse Rodriguez	Andrew	
31			Sylvester I

THE LATIN MASS PRAYERS

(for servers and singers and for use in a
dialogue Mass)

AT THE FOOT OF THE ALTAR

Priest. In nomine Patris et Filii et Spiritus Sancti.
Amen.

Introibo ad altare Dei.

Server. Ad Deum, qui laetificat juventutem meam.

P. Judica me, Deus, et discerne causam meam de
gente non sancta: ab homine iniquo et doloso erue me.

**S. Quia tu es, Deus, fortitudo mea, quare me re-
pulisti? et quare tristis incedo, dum affligit me in-
imicus?**

P. Emitte lucem tuam et veritatem tuam: ipsa me
deduxerunt et adduxerunt in montem sanctum tuum,
et in tabernacula tua.

**S. Et introibo ad altare Dei: ad Deum, qui laetificat
juventutem meam.**

P. Confitebor tibi in cithara, Deus, Deus meus:
quare tristis es anima mea? et quare conturbas me?

**S. Spera in Deo, quoniam adhuc confitebor illi:
salutare vultus mei et Deus meus.**

P. Gloria Patri et Filio et Spiritui Sancto.

**S. Sicut erat in principio, et nunc, et semper, et in
saecula saeculorum. Amen.**

P. Introibo ad altare Dei.

S. Ad Deum, qui laetificat juventutem meam.

P. Adjutorium nostrum in nomine Domini.

S. Qui fecit caelum et terram.

P. Confiteor, etc.

S.   Misereatur tui omnipotens Deus, et dimissis peccatis tuis perducat te ad vitam aeternam.

P.   Amen.

S.   Confiteor Deo omnipotenti, beatae Mariae semper Virgini, beato Michaeli Archangelo, beato Joanni Baptistae, sanctis Apostolis Petro et Paulo, omnibus sanctis, et tibi pater, quia peccavi nimis cogitatione, verbo, et opere: mea culpa, mea culpa, mea maxima culpa.

Ideo precor beatam Mariam semper Virginem, beatum Michaelum Archangelum, beatum Joannem Baptistam, sanctos Apostolos Petrum et Paulum, omnes sanctos, et te pater, orare pro me ad Dominum Deum nostrum.

P.   Misereatur vestri omnipotens Deus et dimissis peccatis vestris perducat vos ad vitam aeternam.

S.   Amen.

P.   Indulgentiam, absolutionem et remissionem peccatorum nostrorum tribuat nobis omnipotens et misericors Dominus.

S.   Amen.

P.   Deus, tu conversus vivificabis nos.

S.   Et plebs tua laetabitur in te.

P.   Ostende nobis, Domine, misericordiam tuam.

S.   Et salutare tuum da nobis.

P.   Domine exaudi orationem meam.

S.   Et clamor meus ad te veniat.

P.   Dominus vobiscum.

S.   Et cum spiritu tuo.

AT THE MIDDLE OF THE ALTAR

P. Kyrie eleison.	S. Kyrie eleison.
P. Kyrie eleison.	S. Christe eleison.
P. Christe eleison.	S. Christe eleison.
P. Kyrie eleison.	S. Kyrie eleison.
P. Kyrie eleison.	

GLORIA

Gloria in excelsis Deo; et in terra pax hominibus bonae voluntatis. Laudamus te; benedicimus te; glorificamus te. Gratias agimus tibi propter magnam gloriam tuam. Domine Deus, Rex caelestis, Deus Pater omnipotens. Domine Fili unigenite, Jesu Christe: Domine Deus, Agnus Dei, Filius Patris, qui tollis peccata mundi, miserere nobis: qui tollis peccata mundi, suscipe deprecationem nostram: qui sedes ad dexteram Patris, miserere nobis. Quoniam tu solus sanctus: tu solus Dominus: tu solus altissimus, Jesu Christe, cum Sancto Spiritu, in gloria Dei Patris. Amen.

AFTER THE GLORIA

P. Dominus vobiscum.

S. **Et cum spiritu tuo.**

P. Oremus ... per omnia saecula saeculorum.

S. **Amen.**

AFTER THE EPISTLE

S. **Deo gratias.**

BEFORE THE GOSPEL

P. Dominus vobiscum.

S. **Et cum spiritu tuo.**

P. Sequentia sancti evangelii secundum ....

S. **Gloria tibi, Domine.**

AFTER THE GOSPEL

S. **Laus tibi, Christe.**

CREDO

Credo in unum Deum, Patrem omnipotentem, factorem caeli et terrae; visibilium omnium et invisibilium. Et in unum Dominum, Jesum Christum, Filium Dei unigenitum, et ex Patre ante omnia saecula. Deum de Deo; Lumen de Lumine; Deum verum de Deo vero; genitum non factum; consubstantialem Patri, per quem omnia facta sunt. Qui propter nos homines, et propter nostram salutem, descendit de caelis, et incarnatus est de Spiritu Sancto, ex Maria Virgine: et homo factus est. Crucifixus etiam pro nobis; sub Pontio Pilato passus et sepultus est. Et resurrexit tertia die secundum scripturas; et ascendit in caelum, sedet ad dexteram Patris: et iterum venturus est cum gloria, judicare vivos et mortuos; cujus regni non erit finis. Et in Spiritum Sanctum, Dominum et vivificantem, qui ex Patre Filioque procedit; qui cum Patre et Filio simul adoratur et conglorificatur; qui locutus est per prophetas. Et unam, sanctam, Catholicam et Apostolicam Ecclesiam. Confiteor unum baptisma in remissionem peccatorum. Et expecto resurrectionem mortuorum et vitam venturi saeculi. Amen.

BEFORE THE OFFERTORY

P. Dominus vobiscum.

S. **Et cum spiritu tuo.**

AFTER THE OFFERTORY

P. Orates fratres . . . .

S. **Suscipiat Dominus sacrificum de manibus tuis ad laudem et gloriam nominis sui, ad utilitatem quoque nostram totiusque ecclesiae suae sanctae.**

AT THE PREFACE

P. Per omnia saecula saeculorum.

S. **Amen.**

P. Dominus vobiscum.

S. **Et cum spiritu tuo.**

P. Sursum corda.

S. **Habemus ad Dominum.**

P. Gratias agamus Domino nostro.

S. **Dignum et justum est.**

END OF THE PREFACE

Sanctus, sanctus, sanctus Dominus Deus Sabaoth. Pleni sunt caeli et terra gloria tua. Hosanna in excelsis. Benedictus, qui venit in nomine Domini. Hosanna in excelsis.

AT THE PATER NOSTER

P. Per omnia saecula saeculorum.

S. **Amen.**

Pater noster, qui es in caelis, sanctificetur nomen tuum: adveniat regnum tuum: fiat voluntas tua sicut in caelo et in terra. Panem nostrum quotidianum da nobis hodie: et dimitte nobis debita nostra, sicut et nos dimittimus debitoribus nostris.

P. Et ne nos inducas in tentationem.

S. **Sed libera nos a malo.**

P. Per omnia saecula saeculorum.

S. **Amen.**

P. Pax Domini sit semper vobiscum.

S. **Et cum spiritu tuo.**

AGNUS DEI

Agnus Dei, qui tollis peccata mundi, miserere nobis.
Agnus Dei, qui tollis peccata mundi, miserere nobis.
Agnus Dei, qui tollis peccata mundi, dona nobis pacem.

AFTER COMMUNION

P. Dominus vobiscum.

S. **Et cum spiritu tuo.**

P. Oremus ... per omnia saecula saeculorum.

S. **Amen.**

P. Dominus vobiscum.

S. **Et cum spiritu tuo.**

P. Ite, missa est (or, Benedicamus Domino).

S. **Deo gratias.**

(Or: P. Requiescant in pace. S. **Amen.**)

P. Benedicat vos omnipotens Deus, Pater et Filius et Spiritus Sanctus.

S. **Amen.**

P. Dominus vobiscum.

S. **Et cum spiritu tuo.**

P. Initium sancti evangelii secundum Joannem.

S. **Gloria tibi, Domine.**

P. In principio, etc.

S. **Deo gratias.**

CPSIA information can be obtained
at www.ICGtesting.com
Printed in the USA
FSOW01n0620180716
22808FS